after
SUFFRAGE

American Politics and Political Economy
A series edited by Benjamin I. Page

after
SUFFRAGE

Women in

Partisan and

Electoral

Politics

before the

New Deal

KRISTI

ANDERSEN

THE UNIVERSITY
OF CHICAGO

CHICAGO AND LONDON

Kristi Andersen is professor of political science at Syracuse University. She is the author of *The Creation of a Democratic Majority, 1928–1936*, also published by the University of Chicago Press.

The University of Chicago Press, Chicago 60637
The University of Chicago Press, Ltd., London
© 1996 by The University of Chicago
All rights reserved. Published 1996
Printed in the United States of America
05 04 03 02 01 00 99 98 97 96   1 2 3 4 5

ISBN: 0-226-01955-1 (cloth)
ISBN: 0-226-01957-8 (paper)

Library of Congress Cataloging-in-Publication Data

Andersen, Kristi.
   After suffrage : women in partisan and electoral politics before
the New Deal / Kristi Andersen.
      p.   cm. — (American politics and political economy)
   Includes bibliographical references (p.   ) and index.
   1. Women in politics—United States—History.   2. United States
—Politics and government—1919–1933.   I. Title.   II. Series.
HQ1236.5.U6A53   1996
320′.082—dc20   95-43395
                                                          CIP

CONTENTS

ACKNOWLEDGMENTS

The genesis of this book was the interdisciplinary project headed by Louise Tilly and Pat Gurin which resulted in the book *Women, Politics, and Change*. Because I had written about the New Deal realignment, and about women's political participation, Louise and Pat mistakenly thought I must know something about women's suffrage and women's politics in the 1920s. I didn't, but my collaboration on this project with a number of notable historians (along with political scientists and sociologists) exposed me to a fascinating period and to a growing literature in women's history. By the time that book was published, I did know something about women's citizenship in the 1920s, but not nearly enough to satisfy myself.

I am thus most grateful to Louise and Pat and to the members of that initial group of collaborators, especially Nancy Cott, Nancy Hewitt, Suzanne Lebsock, Evelyn Brooks Higginbotham, Susan Ware, Jane Mansbridge, Barbara Nelson, and Kay Lehman Schlozman. Sally Kohlstedt, Barbara Farah, and Virginia Sapiro also provided useful comments at early stages of the project.

At Syracuse University, I have presented portions of this work twice to my colleagues in the History department, who have been cordially critical; and to the Gender and Conflict Working Group of the Program for the Analysis and Resolution of Conflict, whose discussion was instrumental in getting me to think in terms of renegotiating gendered boundaries. I have benefited at these presentations and at other times from the comments and suggestions of Bill Stinchcombe, Scott Strickland, Terrie Northrup, Jo Freeman, Eileen McDonagh, Anna Harvey, Elaine Halchin, Bob

McClure, Roberta Sigel, and John Tryneski. And I am grateful to Gayle Boyer who improved the writing immensely.

I was fortunate to have efficient research assistance provided by Jennifer Neel, Nicole Rosmarino, Robin Kolodny, Emily Thorson, and Elaine Halchin; for computer assistance and other kinds of support too numerous to mention, I thank Stuart Thorson.

after
SUFFRAGE

"In the Land of Extinct Volcanoes"
(From *Judge*, 10 May 1913.)

ONE   Suffrage and Political
                     Change

*I have lived to realize the great dream of my life—the enfran-
chisement of women. We are no longer petitioners, we are not
wards of the nation, but free and equal citizens.*

Carrie Chapman Catt, speaking to a celebratory gathering in New York
City after the ratification of the Nineteenth Amendment, 1920.

Woman suffrage was said by its detractors to be a failure. Even its passionate advocates could not help but express some disappointment that suffrage did not produce the accomplishments they had hoped for. Historians and, following them, political scientists who have been interested in women as voters, party members, candidates, and officeholders generally ignored the aftermath of suffrage, implicitly admitting that nothing very interesting happened, with regard to women and electoral politics, until the 1970s.[1]

1. Articles which appeared in the decade after suffrage include some of the "I told you so" variety, e.g., Charles Edward Russell, "Is Woman Suffrage a Failure?" *Century Magazine* 35 (March, 1924); or an article in *Literary Digest* of 1924 titled "Woman Suffrage Declared a Failure." Many supporters of suffrage made interesting and articulate arguments about the "successes" of suffrage, but they often contained an undercurrent of disappointment as well. For example, see Ida M. Tarbell, "Is Woman's Suffrage a Failure?" *Good Housekeeping* 79 (October 1925), 18–19, 237–239; Carrie Chapman Catt "What Women Have Done with the Vote," *Independent* 115 (17 October 1925), 447–48, 456; Florence E. Allen, "The First Ten Years," *Woman's Journal* (August 1930), 5–7, 30–32; Emily Newell Blair, "Are Women a Failure in Politics?" *Harper's Magazine* 151 (June–November 1925), 513–522. Social science analysis during the twenties tended to focus on women's non-voting, the similarity between men's and women's voting, or on women's "conservatism." For examples, see Stuart D. Rice and Malcolm M. Willey, "American Women's Ineffective Use of the Vote," *Current History* 20 (1924): 641–647; William F. Ogburn and Inez Goltra, "How Women Vote," *Political Science Quarterly* 34 (September 1919), 413–433; and Charles E. Merriam and Harold F. Gosnell, *Non-Voting* (Chicago: University of Chicago Press, 1924). The influential works of William ONeill (*Everyone Was Brave* [Chicago: Quadrangle Books, 1969]), and William

This book is an attempt to redress this neglect. It starts with the incontestable facts that, with the advent of woman suffrage, the electorate doubled in size; the political parties at both state and national levels changed their rules, in some cases to include women officials at all levels; and increasing (though still relatively small) numbers of women began running for and holding political offices at all levels. In particular I argue that through an examination of how women and men renegotiated the boundaries that established sex-differentiated roles in the political sphere, we can see how politics was changed by the entry of women into the ranks of voters, party activists, candidates and officeholders. The involvement of women with partisan and electoral (heretofore male) politics after 1920 represents a critical period in the transformation of the relationship between gender and citizenship. In addition, women's political participation (along with their continuing activities in a wide range of voluntary organizations) during this period served as a bridge between Progressivism and the New Deal and helped to solidify the movement from the highly partisan politics of the nineteenth century to the increasingly nonpartisan, candidate-centered, interest group politics of the mid-twentieth century.

GENDER AND CITIZENSHIP

Nancy Cott is correct in arguing that suffrage should not be reified as a "great divide" in women's politics and that the roles and levels of activity of women's voluntary organizations show a great deal of continuity before and after 1920. Moreover, women did sometimes participate in electoral politics before suffrage (and of course by 1920, women in fifteen states already had the right to vote in most elections).[2]

Chafe (*The American Woman: Her Changing Social, Economic and Political Roles, 1920–1970* [New York: Oxford University Press, 1972]) reinforced for later generations the notion that in gaining suffrage women had gained very little.

2. Nancy Cott, "Across the Great Divide: Women in Politics Before and After 1920," in *Women, Politics and Change,* ed. Louise A. Tilly and Patricia Gurin (New York: Russell Sage Foundation, 1990). Sara Monoson's research, for example, describes how women in the Woman's Municipal League in New York City tried to influence the mayoral elections around the turn of the century. S. Sara Monoson, "The Lady and the Tiger: Women's Electoral Activism in New York City Before Suffrage," *Journal of Women's History* 2 (Fall 1990), 100–135.

On the other hand, the attainment of universal female suffrage in the United States represents an important break with the past. The Nineteenth Amendment gave women one fundamental right of democratic citizenship, even though Carrie Chapman Catt's claim (above) that women were now "free and equal citizens" was, as we will see, questionable on many grounds. And certainly if one is concerned primarily with partisan and electoral politics, as I am here, the Nineteenth Amendment is clearly a significant milestone. Suffrage raised the possibility that women would come into main- stream male politics wholesale—that women would vote, cam- paign, and run for office—as well as the possibility that political outcomes would be affected. Equally important, suffrage chal- lenged the assumption of male authority over women, as Ellen Carol DuBois has argued, because the exclusion of women from political power was based on their dependence on men: "woman suffrage constituted a serious challenge to the masculine monopoly of the public sphere. . . . [T]he prospect of enfranchisement was uniquely able to touch all women, offering them a public role and a relation to the community unmediated by husband or children."[3]

During the whole of America's history, woman's citizenship has been defined and constrained by her private roles and functions. Linda Kerber describes vividly the threat that educated, indepen- dent women posed to men in the early Republic, and how this threat was blunted by the emergence of the ideal of the "Republi- can Mother." The "Republican Mother's life was dedicated to the service of civic virtue . . . she educated her sons for it." In this way, "the traditional womanly virtues were endowed with a political purpose."[4] Even as the forms of politics changed during the nine- teenth century, with the rise of popular politics and the increasing centrality of parties in structuring political conflicts, women's citi- zenship remained indirect, mediated by husbands and sons and by an ideology of domesticity. Males, on the other hand, engaged public life directly.

3. Ellen Carol DuBois, *Feminism and Suffrage: The Emergence of an Indepen- dent Women's Movement in America, 1848–1869* (Ithaca: Cornell University Press, 1978), 46–47.
4. Linda K. Kerber, *Women of the Republic: Intellect and Ideology in Revolution- ary America* (Chapel Hill: University of North Carolina Press, 1980), 229–230.

In the nineteenth century, the ideology of domesticity was pushed and stretched to accommodate decidedly unprivate activities. The idea of "municipal housekeeping," for example, which provided support for a vast range of activities undertaken by women's clubs in the late nineteenth century, was essentially a way of legitimating public activities—marches or lobbying, for example—by redefining them under the rubric of women's traditional, "private" concerns with cleanliness, order, and nurture.[5]

By the first two decades of the twentieth century, several trends had combined to make the differences between male and female political cultures, styles, and forms less distinct. First, the assumption that women were physically located primarily in the home was increasingly untenable. The late nineteenth century saw a surge in female employment—for example, the number of women employed as secretaries was about 10,000 in 1870, but 239,000 just thirty years later—and this, in turn, "created a substantial number of women who not only earned money but used their income to exercise the option of living apart from a family group."[6] Public spaces (parks, department stores, restaurants, and streets) were more open to women, and this meant that the distinctions between "good," "respectable," "private" women on the one hand, and "bad" or "public" women on the other, was beginning to break down. Second, the centrality of party and electoral politics was declining; the kinds of political forms, such as lobbying and grassroots educational campaigns, long used by women because they were excluded from electoral and party politics, were now used by men as well.[7] Third, women had at least partial suffrage in a grow-

5. See in particular Ann Firor Scott's recent study of women's associations, *Natural Allies: Women's Organizations in American History* (Urbana: University of Illinois Press, 1991).

6. Glenna Matthews, *The Rise of Public Woman: Woman's Power and Woman's Place in the United States, 1630–1970* (New York: Oxford University Press, 1992), 151–152.

7. Elisabeth S. Clemens, "Organizational Repertoires and Institutional Change: Women's Groups and the Transformation of U.S. Politics, 1890–1920," *American Journal of Sociology* 98 (January 1992), 755–798; Paula Baker, "The Domestication of Politics: Women and American Political Society, 1780–1920," *American Historical Review* 89 (June 1984), 620–647; Michael E. McGerr, "Political Style and Women's Power, 1830–1930," *Journal of American History* 77 (December 1990), 864–885.

ing number of states during this period, and suffragists had dealt with and successfully manipulated the partisan political system to achieve their ends; thus the involvement of women with traditionally male political activities had begun much earlier than 1920.

Nonetheless, women and men from Carrie Chapman Catt to Eleanor Roosevelt believed and argued fervently that important differences, whether inherent or stemming from different experiences, existed between men and women, and in particular characterized their relationship to the public sphere and to politics. An extensive discussion about how women should exercise their newly acquired citizenship rights took place at a time when women were at the point of losing the moral authority that arose from their occupancy of a distinct, private, virtuous space—and when their ability to share in and use power established on a new and egalitarian basis was untested and uncertain.[8]

Women, Politics, and Public Policy in the 1920s

"That woman suffrage had little impact on women or politics has been considered almost axiomatic by historians," claimed Paula Baker in 1984.[9] This view of suffrage has been common since the mid-twenties. Just before the 1924 election and again at the ten-year anniversary of the Nineteenth Amendment, journalists and political pundits produced streams of articles purporting to judge the "success" or "failure" of suffrage. Charles Russell's assertion in 1924 that "nothing has changed, except that the number of docile ballot-droppers has approximately doubled" is often cited as evidence for the lack of change in outcomes. At the same time, the dramatic decline in turnout since 1916 was immediately attributed to women's

---

8. Both Baker ("The Domestication of Politics") and Matthews (*The Rise of Public Woman*, chs. 7 and 8) argue that with suffrage, women lost as well as gained. "In the long run," says Matthews, "as women advanced into 'new' areas, they wound up in another form of woman's sphere, a more circumscribed one" (p. 177). Nancy Cott, in *The Grounding of Modern Feminism* (New Haven: Yale University Press, 1987) has laid out brilliantly the ways that "difference" vs. "equality" describes a persistent tension within early twentieth-century feminist thought and action.

9. Baker, "The Domestication of Politics," 643.

lack of participation.[10] These judgments, in my view, were funda-mentally shaped by certain assumptions: that women and women's political interests and preferences were homogeneous and different from men and men's preferences and that suffrage represented an opportunity that all women would immediately act on. Thus suffrage was judged according to expectations of full participation and sub-stantial change in political outcomes; to the extent that neither hap-pened, suffrage was then judged a failure.

To make a supportable claim that woman suffrage had no im-pact, we must first imagine that the political decisions that were made after women's enfranchisement were made in the same ways, using the same political calculations, as similar decisions made before suffrage. From the point of view of male political elites (members of Congress, state legislatures, county boards and city councils), their constituencies had changed substantially with the addition of millions of new voters. We know from recent research in political science how members of Congress think about constitu-encies and calculate the chances that a position they take will have a detrimental effect on their chances of re-election. This dramatic alteration in their constituencies, given assumptions about gender differences which certainly did not evaporate after suffrage, must have changed their calculations. Since votes were not, with rare exceptions, tallied by sex—and systematic, electorally relevant sur-vey research did not exist until much later—elected officials must have feared the possibility of women acting as a swing vote. This is consistent with the fact that state and local parties, in part based on their histories during the suffrage campaigns, and in part based on the demographic and partisan make-up of the state or locality, varied greatly in the extent to which they welcomed women as activists or candidates and the extent to which they attempted to mobilize women voters.

Second, to argue that woman suffrage had no impact, one would have to claim that the public policies enacted after suffrage would have come into being without woman suffrage. The policy impact

10. Russell, "Is Woman Suffrage a Failure?"; Tarbell, "Is Woman's Suffrage a Failure?"; Rice and Willey, "American Women's Ineffective Use of the Vote."

of woman suffrage has been considered by many historians; the general consensus follows Lemons, who described the early successes attributable to women's efforts (the Shepard-Towner Act and the Cable Act, which addressed women's citizenship) and their later inability to implement change (e.g., the failure to renew the Shepard-Towner Act, which died in 1929) and argued that the change over the course of the decade was due to the fact that men in power realized women were not voting in a bloc and therefore not likely to be able to systematically punish politicians who went against them. William Chafe agrees with Lemons: "Fundamentally . . . women's political standing plummeted [in the latter half of the 1920s] because the mass of female citizens failed to act in the cohesive and committed manner which the suffragists had predicted." Further, he claims, women generally voted "according to their social and economic backgrounds and the political preference of their husbands rather than according to their sex." It is thus implicitly, and sometimes explicitly, assumed that the political failures of some parts of the agenda of organized women's groups in the 1920s were the fault of women—that they were not sufficiently feminist, or politically skilled, unified, or committed.[11] It is interesting that while the 1920s are also commonly seen as a time when the Progressive movement waned, Progressives themselves are only sometimes seen as to blame; more often, explanations are sought in the larger political, social, and economic climate of the times.[12] A similar perspective might help us to reframe our thinking about women's politics in the 1920s. As Carole Nichols says in reference to Connecticut, "If only a portion of their agenda was accepted in the post-suffrage era, it was not for lack of trying. . . . Feminism was inherently antagonistic to the established political order in Connecticut. The women's movement had grown because suffrage leaders endorsed causes of special interest to women—causes which were, in fact, a threat to the control of the state by conserva-

11. J. Stanley Lemons, *The Woman Citizen: Social Feminism in the 1920s* (Urbana: University of Illinois Press, 1973); Chafe, *The American Woman*, 299–300; ONeill, *Everyone Was Brave*, ch. 8.

12. See, for example, Clark A. Chambers, *Seedtime of Reform* (Minneapolis: University of Minnesota Press, 1963).

tive Republicans."[13] Moreover, the stance that woman suffrage had no impact seems at odds with that of the historians who have been painting an increasingly rich and complex picture of the activities of women during this period: their work in voluntary organizations and in the "female dominion" of the social welfare system, their agency in establishing a maternalist welfare state, and their importance in New Deal politics and policymaking.[14] Though the present work can only start on this task, the connections between women active in party and electoral politics, women's organizations, and women involved in implementing national and state social welfare programs must be traced. Most of the scholarly work that concludes that the organized influence of reform-minded women declined during the 1920s looks primarily or wholly at national-level politics and policy. And while state public policy changes reflect in general the same temporal pattern as national policy (more success by women's groups at the first of the decade than later), there has been little attention paid to the political achievements of women's groups at the state level. As one among many examples, Mary M. Thomas describes how the League of Women Voters and other women's groups successfully lobbied the Alabama legislature (which had rejected the suffrage amendment) to pass specific laws allowing women to register, then to accept money

13. Carole Nichols, *Votes and More for Women: Suffrage and After in Connecticut* (New York: Haworth Press, 1983), 3.

14. On voluntary work there is a large literature; see for example Scott, *Natural Allies*; Cott, *The Grounding of Modern Feminism*; Karen Blair, *The Clubwoman as Feminist: True Womanhood Redefined, 1868–1914* (New York: Holmes and Meier, 1980). On the female dominion see Robyn Muncy, *Creating a Female Dominion in American Reform 1890–1935* (New York: Oxford University Press, 1991); Lela Costin, *Two Sisters for Social Justice: A Biography of Grace and Edith Abbot* (Urbana: University of Illinois Press, 1983); Ellen Fitzpatrick, *Endless Crusade: Women Social Scientists and Progressive Reform* (New York: Oxford University Press, 1990). On the "maternalist" state see Theda Skocpol, *Protecting Soldiers and Mothers: The Political Origins of Social Policy in the United States* (Cambridge: Harvard University Press, 1992) and Katherine Kish Sklar, "Historical Foundations of Women's Power in the Creation of the American Welfare State, 1830–1930," in *Mothers of a New World: Maternalist Politics and the Origins of Welfare States* (New York: Routledge, 1993). On women in the New Deal see Susan Ware, *Beyond Suffrage: Women in the New Deal* (Cambridge: Harvard University Press, 1981) and *Partner and I: Molly Dewson, Feminism, and New Deal Politics* (New Haven: Yale University Press, 1987).

through the Shepard-Towner Act and to match that with state funds in order to set up twenty-one health units across the state, and finally to stop the practice of leasing convicts to private industry.[15]

More generally, among a critical mass of women activists, both Democrat and Republican, there was a general consensus on a political agenda which included protective legislation for women and children, women's rights, consumer protection, and industrial health and safety legislation. My discoveries of numerous concrete examples of the efficacy of this consensus (as well as its frequent political failures) reinforced my initial skepticism about the validity of the claim that woman suffrage had no impact. I was convinced, as Suzanne Lebsock was, that "Somewhere between the rhetorical flourishes of the suffragists and the show-me attitude of their detractors lurk possibilities for more interesting ways of posing and answering the questions,"[16] and I have tried to do just that by analyzing the involvement of women in politics between the period of Progressive reform and the advent of the New Deal.

SUFFRAGE AND THE TRANSFORMATION OF AMERICAN POLITICS

Between Susan B. Anthony's work for women's rights in the mid-nineteenth century and the attainment of suffrage seventy years later, the American political system had been transformed. In the place of voter turnouts approaching 90%, the vote had been on a steady decline since 1896. Parties no longer had absolute preeminence in structuring the political environment, as had been the case since the Jacksonian era. In contrast to the opprobrium directed against men without party loyalty in the last century, there was growing respect for the independent voter who chose "the man, not the party." Civil service reforms had reduced party patronage. The organization and mechanics of elections were no longer controlled primarily by parties; Progressive reforms includ-

15. Mary Martha Thomas, *The New Woman in Alabama: Social Reforms and Suffrage, 1890–1920* (Tuscaloosa: University of Alabama Press, 1992).
16. Suzanne Lebsock, "Women and American Politics, 1880–1920," in *Women, Politics and Change*, ed. Louise A. Tilly and Patricia Gurin (New York: Russell Sage Foundation, 1990), 56.

ing voter registration, the Australian ballot, and the direct primary meant increased state control of parties and voting.

The sources of these changes are the subject of contention and of a great deal of research by political scientists and historians.[17] The specific parts played by women, by arguments about woman suffrage, and by the change in the political universe represented by suffrage itself are difficult to untangle. But the changes in the larger political system and the changes associated with woman suffrage are certainly not independent of one another.

One political phenomenon that has been conventionally connected to woman suffrage is the severe drop-off in voter turnout that occurred in the 1920s. Paul Kleppner has used turnout trends from years previous to women's suffrage to predict turnout levels in the 1920s; this allows him to measure the relative contribution of female suffrage and other factors to the low turnout rates of the 1920s. He concludes that "the lack of consistent results across states belies the sufficiency of a 'female suffrage' explanation." Instead, the explanation lies in the larger political system: "[The] geographically extensive Republican hegemony could not fail to have had an impact on electoral turnout. . . . These were the political-environmental conditions that prevailed when most women were initially enfranchised. Politics generally lacked its earlier intensity and strong voter stimulus. . . . If for newly or recently enfranchised women the impact of weaker political stimuli was greater than for men, that was because their costs of participation were higher—they had to overcome standing and internalized norms that defined their sex roles as apolitical."[18]

17. A few of the most important are Walter Dean Burnham, "The System of 1896: An Analysis," in *The Evolution of American Electoral Systems*, ed. Paul Kleppner (Westport, CT: Greenwood Press, 1981) and "Theory and Voting Research: Some Reflections on Converse's 'Change in the American Electorate,'" *American Political Science Review* 68 (1974), 1002–23; Philip E. Converse, "Change in the American Electorate," in *The Human Meaning of Social Change*, ed. Angus Campbell and Philip E. Converse (New York: Russell Sage, 1972); Jerrold G. Rusk, "The Effect of the Australian Ballot Reform on Split Ticket Voting, 1876–1908," *American Political Science Review* 64 (December 1970), 1220–38; John F. Reynolds, *Testing Democracy* (Chapel Hill: University of North Carolina Press, 1988); Michael McGerr, *The Decline of Popular Politics*.

18. Paul Kleppner, "Were Women to Blame? Female Suffrage and Voter Turnout," *Journal of Interdisciplinary History* 12 (Spring 1982), 641, 643.

In this instance, in other words, a focus on the easy explanation—woman suffrage—obscures the fact that other changes in the political universe were acting to depress voter participation. Political scientists and party historians commonly look at the 1920s as the final decade of the System of 1896, or the fourth party system, which was solidified with McKinley's defeat of William Jennings Bryan in 1896. One of the results of this realignment was a dramatic increase in political sectionalism: Democrats dominated the South and Republicans controlled many areas in the Northeast and Midwest. The resulting lack of competition in many areas reduced turnout. Progressive goals of reforming and "rationalizing" politics resulted in the enactment of state registration laws, which in combination with literacy tests, poll taxes and other Jim Crow Laws further constricted the size of the electorate.[19]

The periodicity of realignments can be explained in part by the fact that different political generations have varied levels of attachments to parties. More specifically, those citizens who are of voting age (particularly those who have just entered the electorate) during the intensely polarized years of a party realignment will have strong party identifications, whereas those of their children will be weaker. Children of parents who came of age before the most recent realignment—before the period of increased interest, clear choices, and intense focus that characterizes any realignment period—will have the weakest attachments to parties. From this perspective the electorate of the 1920s was heavily populated with citizens who had no intense loyalty to parties; this lack of partisan moorings was accentuated by the large numbers of newly enfranchised immigrants and children of immigrants who also had no tradition of party attachments in the United States.[20] Thus the decrease in party competition, patterns of immigration, changes in electoral laws, and the generational distance from the realignment of 1896 all would lead us to expect low turnout in the 1920s, independent of woman suffrage.

19. Walter Dean Burnham, "The Changing Shape of the American Political Universe," *American Political Science Review* 59 (March 1965), 7–28.
20. Paul Allen Beck, "A Socialization Theory of Partisan Realignment," in *Controversies in American Voting Behavior*, ed. Richard Niemi and Herbert Weisberg (San Francisco: W. H. Freeman, 1976) and Kristi Andersen, *The Creation of a Democratic Majority, 1928–1936* (Chicago: University of Chicago Press, 1979).

At the same time, other less measurable but equally important changes in American political culture may owe a good deal to the incorporation of women into the voting citizenry. As one example, both the transfer of polling places from barrooms and barber shops to more gender-neutral civic establishments such as schools or churches and the introduction of the Australian ballot played a role in the transformation of voting from a celebratory ritual affirming one's partisan identity to a more individualistic, reflective act. Another example of the way that woman suffrage interacted with other political changes is discussed by John Reynolds in the context of the 1920 election in New Jersey. The election was widely judged to be the "cleanest" and "quietest" in memory, and as he points out this change toward a more subdued electoral environment must have predated suffrage (and, he argues elsewhere, the changed climate actually helped suffrage seem unthreatening and even "inevitable"). On the other hand, the newly formed League of Women Voters, by sponsoring debates between opposing candidates (instead of rallies as the old party organizations used to), helped to shift the focus toward candidates at the expense of party enthusiasm and unity.[21]

Suffrage, and in this I include the suffrage movement, the Amendment itself, and the political activities of women which it facilitated, played an important role in the evolving System of 1896. My purpose here is to place the changes that accompanied woman suffrage into the larger context of the systemic changes taking place at the same time.

MEN AND WOMEN "DOING POLITICS": CHANGING BOUNDARIES

If politics—the institutions and practices by which collective decisions are made for a society—represents the most public of spaces, it is easy to see why women, traditionally confined to the private world of home and family, have long been excluded. Aristotle described the *polis* as "the most sovereign and inclusive association" and the citizen of the *polis* as "a man who shares in the administra-

21. Reynolds, *Testing Democracy*, 163–64.

tion of justice and in the holding of office."[22] The *polis* was composed of private households, including in addition to the male citizens wives, children, and slaves; these households existed essentially to provide the "necessary conditions" for free male citizens to participate fully in public life. This strict division of social life into public and private, and the unbreakable association of those spheres with male and female, probably has not existed since the ancient Greeks, if it existed then. Nonetheless, the realm of politics has been consistently seen as the domain of men, despite numerous situations in which women have been able to play important political roles.[23]

Certainly nineteenth-century American politics, as then culturally defined, was an almost exclusively male activity. Not only were officeholders virtually all male, not only was suffrage denied to women in most places and in most elections, but men were the participants in the rallies, parades, picnics, speeches and campaigns of popular politics. Women "played a limited role in the man's world of popular politics. Not surprisingly, women prepared the food and decorated the halls for rallies. Girls presented flags and banners to marching companies and dressed as the 'Goddess of Liberty' to salute passing parades."[24]

Women's sphere included voluntary and charitable activities of all kinds, which were assumed to spring from women's more virtuous, moral, and selfless natures. Their "moral nature" (as well as an increase in leisure time, especially for white middle-class urban women) propelled them first into benevolent societies and self-improvement clubs, later into organizations focused on "municipal housekeeping." Women in the nineteenth century used demonstrations, petitions, and boycotts in addition to lobbying, pamphlets, and persuasion, while in many states women had been able to vote, at least in school board elections or other local elections, long before the Nineteenth Amendment was ratified, and a few

22. Ernest Baker, ed. and trans., *The Politics of Aristotle* (New York: Oxford University Press, 1962), bk. 1, sec. A.1, and bk. 3, sec. A.1.

23. For perhaps the best discussion of the exclusion of women from politics, see Susan Muller Okin, *Women in Western Political Thought* (Princeton: Princeton University Press, 1979); also Matthews, *The Rise of Public Woman*, and Jean Bethke Elshtain, *Public Man, Private Woman* (Princeton: Princeton University Press, 1981).

24. McGerr, *The Decline of Popular Politics*, 298.

held office at local levels.[25] Nonetheless, since all women did not have the vote and women rarely worked through the political parties, their activities in the public were considered outside of politics, really "above" politics—even tactics such as lobbying or petitioning, which we would place squarely within today's definition of politics.[26]

Many of the arguments against woman suffrage demonstrate a fear that the distinction between public man and private woman would be blurred, to the detriment of the family and the society. Anti-suffragists argued that the vote would divert women from their true and holy function of caring for household, family and husband. And to the extent that the society was composed of households (much like Aristotle's *polis*), what threatened the security and smooth functioning of the household also threatened the society.[27] Opponents of suffrage certainly asserted—somewhat desperately, it often seems in retrospect—that being in-

25. At the same time, men—particularly those who supported the cause of Progressivism—were concerned about many of the same issues championed by the women's organizations. See for example Baker, "The Domestication of Politics"; McGerr, "Political Style and Women's Power"; and Carl Degler, *At Odds: Women and the Family in America from the Revolution to the Present* (New York: Oxford University Press, 1980), 336–339. A further problem with taking the notion of "separate spheres" too literally is raised by Jacqueline Jones, who argues that the worlds inhabited by middle-class white men and women had little relevance to "black women whose status was defined first and foremost (in the eyes of whites) by the labor they performed. Jacqueline Jones, "The Political Implications of Black and White Women's Work in the South, 1890–1965," in *Women, Politics and Change*, ed. Louise A. Tilly and Patricia Gurin (New York: Russell Sage Foundation, 1990), 111. Linda Kerber's article, "Separate Spheres, Female Worlds, Woman's Place: The Rhetoric of Women's History," *Journal of American History* 75 (June 1988), 9–39, offers an insightful critique of the metaphor of separate spheres.

26. An interesting illustration of the extreme of the "separate spheres" perspective is the Women's Parliament, which was convened in New York City in 1869. The idea behind the Parliament was to create a kind of parallel government to deal with issues of social policy of particular concern to women. The members of the Women's Parliament did not, however, support women's suffrage; it was seen as a threat to the separation of male, partisan politics from the moralistic female political culture. See Baker, "The Domestication of Politics," 633–34, and Karen Blair, *The Clubwoman as Feminist*, 39–45.

27. See Chafe, *The American Woman*, ch. 1; O'Neill, *Everyone Was Brave*; and Aileen S. Kraditor, *The Ideas of the Woman Suffrage Movement, 1890–1920* (New York: Columbia University Press, 1965).

volved in politics would change women for the worse or sully their purity.

Women's involvement in partisan and electoral (male) politics after 1920 helped to redefine the boundaries between male and female—particularly in the way that boundary determined what was expected or acceptable male and female activity in the public sphere.[28] Just as feminist historians have looked at the way gender boundaries in education, the professions, and business changed during this period, I look at politics as a profession or occupation or avocation which had its own norms and expectations and which necessarily changed, after 1920, to include (some) women. As I discuss in chapters 4 and 5, how the women who chose to enter male politics tried to renegotiate the boundaries is an important question; how was "women's space" in politics defined? Biographies of women who were involved in electoral politics during this period, newspaper accounts of political conflicts surrounding women's entry into politics, and more recent studies of women in the period after suffrage all provide insights into the processes of domination and negotiation that shifted the boundaries in the arena of conventional politics.

Recent works have investigated similar changes in boundaries during this same period. Business, Sharon Strom writes, was being

---

28. The framework I use here, which is based on the concepts of gender-based boundaries, challenges to boundaries as a result of gender consciousness, and changes in boundaries as a result of reciprocal negotiation, comes from Judith M. Gerson and Kathy Piess, "Boundaries, Negotiation, Consciousness: Reconceptualizing Gender Relations," *Social Problems* 32 (1985), 317–331. The concept of boundaries gets around the problems associated with assuming universalistic, separate men's and women's "spheres." Thus there may be, in a particular historical and social context, boundaries dividing men and women's leisure time activities, while boundaries of a different sort produce sex divisions in the workplace. In the latter instance we can see that while some important boundaries may be permeable (now women are admitted to medical schools and there are significant numbers of women physicians, for example), other boundaries will still exist, or new sub-boundaries will be established (there may be medical specialties which are more or less sex-specific; there may be sex-specific "rules" about interpersonal behavior such as touch or naming). Boundaries are not only potentially permeable or changeable, but are negotiable. This way of understanding the changing dynamics of male-female relationships allows for a more precise specification of how resources are used by men and women in bargaining about changes in privileges and opportunities.

transformed in the first three decades of the twentieth century by growth, increasing complexity, and new theories of management. "As far as early business professionals were concerned, women and feminine influence had to be excluded from the managerial ethos or its masculine purity would be threatened." But by the 1920s, Taylorism and "scientific management" were also affected by the disciplines of psychology and personnel management. This may have threatened the "male managerial ethos," but it also provided a separate place for women within business: "If women found it nearly impossible to enter engineering and the best graduate schools of business administration, they could certainly become psychologists, and psychologists could become employment experts and even personnel managers." Resistance to these changes came from many sources, including William H. Leffingwell, Taylor's counterpart in the field of office management, who thought that more women in offices meant lower standards. Gendered categories of office work helped to maintain sexual difference, and to keep women "assisting" rather than "directing" men. "Employers sought to designate routine clerical work as 'light manufacturing,' to associate it with women's operative status in factories, and to suggest that while it was appropriate for most women it was not in any way similar to the skilled work of most men."[29]

Politics was the site of similar changes in gendered boundaries. As the ratification of the suffrage amendment finally and fully erased one important technical boundary between men and women, others remained in place. The woman suffrage movement, by and large, had not mentioned that the right to vote might entail the right to hold office, though suffragists had talked extensively about whether or not to participate in party politics. Several states decided that gaining the vote did not imply that women had a right to hold office; some did not modify their constitutions to allow the election of women to state legislatures until the 1940s. The parties were quick to give women nominal equality with the male officials and activists in the parties, at least at the national level and in some cases at the state level. The number of women at the party

29. Sharon Hartman Strom, *Beyond the Typewriter: Gender, Class, and the Origins of Modern American Office Work, 1900–1930* (Urbana: University of Illinois Press, 1992), 5–6.

conventions in 1920 soared. However, as I discuss in chapter 4, resistance to these changes was widespread, and their implementation was a long process of negotiation and frequently bitter compromise, from the point of view of women. The number of women serving in state legislatures grew to 146 by 1931, and female officeholders at the local level were relatively common by the end of the decade, where they had been extremely rare before 1920. Here, too, as chapter 5 illustrates, new boundaries were constructed once women were allowed inside political institutions such as Congress and state legislatures. Women were expected to remain womanly, to avoid displaying political ambition, and to be interested primarily in a narrow range of women's issues—a definition of the bounds of women's place in politics that has only come under sustained attack in the past twenty-five years.[30]

Most of the characters in the story of woman suffrage are white, middle-class women. Suffragists sometimes used anti-black and anti-immigrant arguments to advance their cause, and this rhetoric reflected the reality of a substantially white and middle-class movement. During the decade after suffrage, the women who became actively involved in party politics and who ran for office tended to have had backgrounds in the suffrage movement, in the League of Women Voters, and in a variety of women's clubs and organizations, and thus tended to reflect this same bias. Though I have tried to describe briefly the racial and class variation in women's mobilization and to deal briefly with the way that the parties treated African-American women, their story is told much more completely by scholars such as Evelyn Brooks Higginbotham and Rosalyn Terborg-Penn.[31]

30. For a thorough and insightful discussion of the "political integration" of women, see Virginia Sapiro, *The Political Integration of Women: Roles, Socialization, and Politics* (Urbana: University of Illinois Press, 1983).

31. Evelyn Brooks Higginbotham, "In Politics to Stay: Black Women Leaders and Party Politics in the 1920s," in *Women, Politics and Change*, ed. Louise A. Tilly and Patricia Gurin (New York: Russell Sage Foundation, 1990); Rosalyn M. Terborg-Penn, "Discontented Black Feminists: Prelude and Postscript to the Passage of the Nineteenth Amendment," in *Decades of Discontent: The Women's Movement, 1920–1940*, ed. Lois Scharf and Joan M. Jensen (Westport, CT: Greenwood Press, 1983).

The book's organization moves from the margins to the center of electoral politics. First, the discourse about the relationship between gender and public life, especially as it was played out around the time of suffrage in arguments about politics, parties, and women's proper role, is discussed in chapter 2. In chapter 3, I consider women in the 1920s as voters, presenting evidence about the gradual socialization of women into participatory politics and attempting to explain why some groups of new women citizens were much more likely to vote than others. Chapter 4 tells a small part of the story of women's involvement in the political parties. As self-interested organizations motivated primarily by a desire to maximize votes, parties reacted quickly to the expansion of the electorate, making organizational and public relations changes designed to mobilize women voters. At the same time, the responses of male party leaders and activists to women's demands clearly illustrates their resistance to allowing women into this male domain. Chapter 5 looks at women as candidates and officeholders during the decade of the 1920s, mapping out the offices that were beginning to be acceptable for women to hold, and again documenting the resistance to the idea and the reality of female politicians. The last chapter returns to a discussion of the impact that woman suffrage had on ideas about gender and citizenship; on changes in party politics and policy outcomes; on the ongoing transformation of the political system; and on how political people behaved and how they described what they were doing in the period after suffrage.

A final note: one of the problems with writing about any sort of social change, or at least social change which you value or advocate, is whether to present the glass as half-empty or half-full. Particularly because so many popular and scholarly views of the 1920s assume that suffrage was a failure, it seems both necessary and desirable to point out the changes that occurred, subsequent to the Nineteenth Amendment, in both women's political roles and in the substance and form of politics. On the other hand, the constraints that were imposed on women as they sought to gain real political power are equally important, and must be carefully described and explained. Sharon Strom, in her recent book about women and office work, describes a similar dilemma when trying to decide "whether the woman office clerk was taking advantage of new opportunities for the working woman or whether she was just another version of exploited female labor." Her solution: the answers to both questions are "yes."[32] Similarly, I believe it makes sense to reconsider women's involvement in electoral and party politics in the 1920s as producing transformations that would not reach fruition for many years, at the same time that resistance to change on the part of male party and political leaders severely limited the amount of change which could take place—a limitation that political women in the 1920s clearly recognized.

32. Strom, *Beyond the Typewriter*, 2.

"Always an Uncomfortable Season of the Year for the Men Folks"

TWO   Expanding Women's Citizenship in the 1920s

*V*oting is not a right, but a duty; not a privilege refused to women, but a task from which she has been exempt in the past . . . The question for the woman is not, have I a right to share in the privilege of governing the State? but, is it my duty to take up the task of governing the State? The primary object of government is to protect persons and property: is it the duty of women to share with men in protecting the persons and property of the community? No one supposes that she should perform military, policy, or fireman's duty . . . few suppose that she should act as sheriff, mayor, governor, judge or legislator. Ought she, then, to assume the responsibilities of government, but not its difficulties and hazards? To arrest no one, but to direct the police whom to arrest? . . . A ballot is not an expression of opinion; it is a command.

. . . The women can always exert an influence more powerful in all parties because they belong to none. . . . and they keep alive in the hearts of men ideals of political action just because they do not have to consider what are the immediate practical steps toward their realization.

Rev. Lyman Abbott,
"Why the Vote Would Be Injurious to Women," 1910 [1]

T he debate over woman suffrage revolved around questions of how women should be connected to civil society; it raised more general questions about republican citizenship. The arguments among the suffragists themselves over how women should exercise their new citizenship rights also revolved around questions of whether women's relationship to the polity

1. This was one of a series of articles representing different opinions on woman suffrage. *Ladies Home Journal* 27 (February 1910), 21–22.

should be based on a moral stance unique to women. One way to organize these ideas is to focus on the tension between equality and difference, as do Nancy Cott and Aileen Kraditor.[2] This tension does serve as background and context for the discussion in this chapter, but I have chosen to focus first on what Linda Kerber calls the "different variants" of republicanism prescribed for men and women in the nineteenth and early twentieth centuries. The connections between citizenship (in its gendered variations) and voting, party loyalty, and officeholding will then be examined. Finally, within this broader context of American ideas about citizenship and the connections between citizenship and day-to-day political behavior, I will analyze the arguments that took place among women—primarily suffragists and activists—as to the ways that women should act to expand their citizenship after suffrage.

MALE AND FEMALE CITIZENS

During the whole of American history, the dominant political culture has established distinct expectations for male and female Americans. We have every reason to believe that Tocqueville's observations about the separation of male and female spheres resonated in the lives of ordinary people, who believed that men and women made very different contributions to civil society. For the Revolutionary generation, the idea of "Republican motherhood" (as Linda Kerber has described it) offered one solution to the dilemma presented by the heritage of classical republicanism, which valued equality but whose notion of citizenship presumed

2. Nancy Cott, *The Grounding of Modern Feminism,* and Aileen Kraditor, *The Ideas of the Woman Suffrage Movement.* Kraditor's book is the classic study of the ideologies used by the suffrage movement. Rather than the terms equality and difference, she distinguishes between arguments based on "equality" and "expediency." Expediency arguments are based on the notion that women's unique skills and concerns would benefit the polity. In a recent article, Wendy Sarvasy argues that applying this dualism to the National Women's Party and the "social feminists" of the 1920s obscures the fact that both can be seen as looking for a "theoretical and practical synthesis of equality and difference as the basis for women's citizenship." Both were trying to design a "feminist welfare state." Wendy Sarvasy, "Beyond the Difference versus Equality Policy Debate: Postsuffrage Feminism, Citizenship, and the Quest for a Feminist Welfare State," *Signs* 17 (Winter 1992), 335.

the ability to bear arms in defense of the republic, and thus effectively excluded women.[3] Republican mothers, who inculcated their sons with civic virtues, ensured citizens' commitment to the good of the republic, but their own connection to public life was, obviously, indirect. At the same time, "consciousness of their civic obligation also meant that old boundaries on women's lives were stretched. . . . In this way, Republican motherhood could also sustain a major step in the direction of a liberal individualism which recognized the political potential of women."[4]

The concept of Republican motherhood incorporates two themes that continued to shape ideas about women's citizenship through the nineteenth century and into the twentieth. *Disinterestedness*, or unselfish public-mindedness, is as Kerber reminds us, one language of American politics, a language inherited from the Florentines that stresses participation and virtue.[5] The other language was that of Lockean liberal individualism, a heritage "preoccupied with private rights."[6] If self-interested behavior in politics and in the marketplace was thought to be productive of the public good, the disinterested, virtuous citizen of the Jeffersonian vision would be unnecessary. Women, however, who could not control property, were independent of (and uncorrupted by) the selfish motivations that were the engine of the market, and thus retained a moral authority based precisely on their disinterestedness. In addition, women's connection to the public arena was through their family: women's membership in the community was characterized by its *indirectness*, as it was not based on a woman's individual

3. The argument that women could not participate fully in civic life because they were presumed unable to bear arms or to "protect" society was still used to argue against suffrage, as is clear from the quote used to introduce this chapter.

4. Linda Kerber, "The Republican Ideology of the Revolutionary Generation," *American Quarterly* 37 (fall 1985), 474–95. See also Kerber's more extensive discussion of Republican motherhood in *Women of the Republic*.

5. Glenna Matthews quotes from Abigail Adams' letter to her husband to illustrate the widespread idea of female disinterestedness as an important civic virtue: "Patriotism in the female Sex is the most disinterested of all virtues. Excluded from honour and from offices . . . our property is subject to the controls and disposal of our partners, . . . Yet all History and every age exhibit Instances of patriotical virtue in the female Sex" (Matthews, *The Rise of Public Woman*, 65–66).

6. Kerber, "The Republican Ideology of the Revolutionary Generation," 485–86.

rights but on her functions as mother, wife, and homemaker. The contributions that she was expected to make to the collectivity were based on these obligations.

The unique position of women, at one remove from public life, reinforced the idea that politics was the domain of men. Thus the civic virtues assigned to private women were quite different from those assigned to public men. Paula Baker's careful study of public life in rural New York in the late nineteenth and early twentieth centuries offers a clear picture of the very different connections to the polity that were characteristic of men and women. Men found their public voice through politics, and this was universally assumed to mean *electoral* politics—voting and holding office. Politics in turn was linked to ideas of specifically male virtues and capabilities. Male attributes or manliness—courage, loyalty, integrity, self-assertion, and friendship—were seen as worthy of public reward and were thus the basis for praising candidates and officeholders. Successful candidates were routinely praised for their manliness, while those who deserted their political friends or their parties were criticized as being less than manly, or in one instance as being "political hermaphrodites." When men wrote letters to public officials to ask for favors or support, they invoked the norms of political friendship, a kind of exchange relationship, because they had resources (connections with other men, votes) with which to negotiate.[7]

Rural women, on the other hand, found themselves in quite a different situation. They found it much more difficult to become involved in organizations—distance, dependence on men for transportation, and the hard work that was their lot prevented them from creating and sustaining the same sorts of organizations that attracted their urban sisters. The groups that did exist were mostly associated with churches, and typically focused their energies on helping their own needy members—perhaps people in the church who had lost their jobs or had their house destroyed by a fire. Other efforts of these groups sent material or monetary donations to urban areas or to missions abroad. Women also, argues Baker, tended to see the state government as a potential ally, whereas

7. Paula Baker, *The Moral Frameworks of Public Life: Gender, Politics, and the State in Rural New York* (New York: Oxford University Press), ch. 2.

men in rural New York "saw state government as overly partisan and expensive and as the source of policies that benefited only rich urban men."[8] Women's letters to officeholders asking for favors differed substantially from men's. Because women had nothing to trade—no vote, no political friendship or political support—they apologized for taking the time of the reader, claimed that the favors they asked would benefit others, and/or communicated their dire need. "More than a confirmation of the writers' femininity, the apologetic tone of womens letters showed that women negotiated for politicians' favors from a position of weakness."[9]

Piety and domesticity (which were expressed in these letters as well as through women's church work) were important in the female construction of public values. These values helped to define further male and female politics. "By applying standards of moral righteousness and correctness to certain issues, women concerned with partisan politics found it difficult to identify with the major political parties."[10] The women of the Woman's Municipal League in New York at the turn of the century chose not to link a candidate's stand on suffrage to support for his campaign (even though the League's founder was a supporter) because "both the League members and their male allies considered linking these issues to be in conflict with women's claim to be nonpartisan, disinterested advocates of reform."[11] The women wanted to avoid the appearance of operating on a quid pro quo basis, the foundation of men's interest-based politics.

Just as strongly, virtually all women felt the need to distinguish their activities from "politics." When they were involved in elec-

---

8. Baker, *The Moral Frameworks of Public Life*, 80. Maureen Flanagan, who compares the City Club and the Womans City Club of Chicago during the Progressive era, also finds a clear difference between the stances of male and female organizations toward government: while the City Club remained "solidly on the side of private profit and limited municipal power over city services," the Woman's City Club believed that "municipal problems required solutions that guaranteed the well-being of everyone within the city," and this often led them to advocate more government responsibility and control. Maureen A. Flanagan, "Gender and Urban Political Reform: The City Club and the Woman's City Club of Chicago in the Progressive Era," *American Historical Review* 95 (October 1990), 1032–50.
9. Baker, *The Moral Frameworks of Public Life*, 87.
10. Baker, *The Moral Frameworks of Public Life*, 82.
11. Monoson, "The Lady and the Tiger," 101.

toral politics, like the Woman's Municipal League, they "attempted
to redefine the proper business of (municipal) politics" by claiming
(in common with many male Progressives) that the work of municipal governments was properly nonpartisan and therefore nonpolitical.[12] Thus women, who were not "in politics," could be involved
in reform and, as Monoson's research shows, even in elections.
The progression toward involvement in government policymaking
and sometimes in electoral politics is well documented in Anne
Scott's study of women's associations. For example, the Mothers'
Club of Cambridge began, in 1878, to discuss problems of raising
children and keeping a home—essentially a self-improvement
club. "Sometime in the early nineties the minutes began to reflect
a subtle change in direction," says Scott. "Increasingly programs
included papers with titles such as 'The Need of a District Nurse
in Cambridge,' 'The Tenement House,' or 'An Eight-Hour Law.'"
The club discussed trying to elect some of their members to the
School Committee and decided to learn about local government.
Around the turn of the century, they not only lobbied for legislation
they supported, but also began projects such as vacation schools
and playgrounds. Repeatedly, the club would begin a program and,
when the community was ready to support it, would turn over
responsibility to local governments.[13] But referring to their activities as "municipal housekeeping" (a term popularized by Jane Addams, among others), they "conferred an air of respectability upon
what might otherwise have been considered unseemly public or
political activity."[14] A good example of this expansive tendency can
be found in Scott's description of El Paso, where women formed
a Child Culture Study Circle, which was transformed eventually
into the Civic Improvement League. By 1914 a local newspaper
asserted that the League was doing more for "civic betterment"
than any other organization.[15] Nonetheless, as Scott's phrase "unseemly public or political activity" indicates, the distinction be-

12. *Ibid.*
13. Scott, *Natural Allies,* 123–26; Sarah Deutsch, "Learning to Talk More Like
a Man: Boston Women's Class-Bridging Organizations, 1870–1940, *American Historical Review* 97 (April 1992): 379–404.
14. Scott, *Natural Allies,* 142.
15. Scott, *Natural Allies,* 144–45.

tween what men could do and what women could do in the public arena remained clear for most people, even though, almost invisibly, the boundary was being redefined. Even as the Nineteenth Amendment neared ratification, women were still reluctant to think of themselves as being political or in politics. When the New York City League of Women Voters sent out questionnaires to candidates in 1919, one woman replied to a question about how long she had been in politics, "In the generally accepted sense never was, am not now, and never will be."[16]

These models of male and female citizenship had several implications for women who would soon have the right to vote and, with it, the potential to be involved in party politics and campaigns, serve on juries, and run for office. Women's activities were not seen as political, even if we would classify them as such today. Also, the illusion that women did not have *selfish* interests was widespread, as can be seen in many of the arguments for suffrage. Because women did not have (or were presumed not to have) a direct connection to the market or the polity as individuals, they were not characterized by the kinds of "interests" that since Madison's day have been seen as motivating political choices. Rather, their concerns revolved around protecting their homes, children, families, and communities. Women were also assumed to be generally more moral, more delicate, and less corruptible than men.

Once the issue of suffrage was apparently resolved, a range of ideas about women's citizenship began to emerge. Whether voting rights implied other rights constituted one discussion; the fact that this was contentious illustrates the persistence of gendered ideas of citizenship. For example, it quickly became clear that women were still in a special category with regard to retaining their U.S. citizenship. The Cable Act of 1922, which allowed women to remain citizens if they married foreigners (though such women were considered naturalized citizens), needed strong efforts by the Women's Joint Congressional Committee (a coalition of women's organizations) to pass. Nor did the right to serve on juries follow directly from the right to vote, though many women assumed it

16. *Woman Citizen,* 20 September 1919, 401. *The Woman Citizen* changed its name later in the decade to *The Woman's Journal* and ceased publication in 1931.

would or should. When pressed, in the 1920s and 1930s, many states ruled that the Nineteenth Amendment applied solely to voting and did not confer other rights or obligations of citizenship. Some state constitutions were not amended to allow the election of women to legislative offices until the 1940s.[17] Of course, even when women were allowed to serve on juries, gendered boundaries remained. The first all-woman jury "east of the Alleghenies" was impaneled in New Jersey District Court in 1920. All agreed that they handled their "novel duties" with ease and the judge asserted that he would be calling more women as jurors in the future. "The only cases I shall not give them will be those involving slander, where they might be forced to hear bad language."[18]

Though there was little agreement on how the right to vote would affect these other rights, it seems clear that the fact that women could now vote in large numbers made it *more likely* that their rights to retain citizenship, serve on juries, and hold office would be conceded to them. After the passage of the Cable Act, one congressman said that in his judgment, "there was no particular force in the demand for this bill until the Nineteenth Amendment became a part of the organic law of the land."[19] Florence E. Allen, at the time an Ohio State Supreme Court justice, summarized the argument about the relationship between the right to vote and other rights: "Whether or not the ballot is exercised at all, whether or not it is exercised foolishly, there is a potential power in the franchise which makes its holder more influential than the one who does not have the vote. . . . [The voting right] carries with it other vital rights all along the line."[20]

CITIZENSHIP, PARTY, AND VOTING

Beyond issues of rights, however, the interesting questions had to do with how women's values of domesticity, piety, distinterested-

17. Lemons, *The Woman Citizen*, 68–73; Anne Williams Wheaton, "The Woman Voter," *The Woman's Journal* (February 1929), 28.

18. *New York Times*, 14 October 1920, p. 1.

19. *Congressional Record*, 87th Congress, 2d sess., 62:-9047. Cited in Lemons, *The Woman Citizen*, 66.

20. Allen, "The First Ten Years," 6.

ness, and nonpartisanship fit into a political system based on partisanship, ambition, and competing interests.

Aside from the four western states where women had been enfranchised in the nineteenth century, women acquired the right to vote (in eleven states between 1900 and 1920, then universally after the ratification of the Nineteenth Amendment) during a period when the emphatically partisan politics of the nineteenth century were giving way to a political system more open to interest groups, where partisan identity counted for less and party organizations had fewer resources at their disposal. Consistent with this, Paula Baker argues that "woman suffrage was adopted just at the time when the influence of parties and electoral politics on public policy was declining,"[21] and though this is easy for us to see in hindsight, it was not so clear to women and men at the time. The leaders of the suffrage movement had, after all, spent their formative years in a political culture that was aggressively and universally partisan, and frequently asserted that parties were central to politics, and that only by working through the parties could one engage the levers of change.

I am thus arguing that we must understand the important features of the nineteenth-century political universe, as well as the changes that occurred during the Progressive era, in order to understand the thinking of women suffragists and activists at the time of suffrage. Historian Joel Silbey describes the American political system after 1820 in this way: "In this extraordinarily partisan age of American politics, from the 1830s to the 1890s, individual and group party loyalty was deep, intense, powerful and persistent. . . . Party organizations worked primarily to arouse those already committed."[22]

Each local party organization put on speeches, rallies, barbecues, and other entertainment during the campaigns, canvassed its supporters, provided them all with pre-printed ballots (or "tickets"), saw that voters got to the polls and often sponsored election-day festivities. As this latter point may indicate, "One did not simply

21. Baker, "The Domestication of Politics," 645.
22. Joel Silbey, "Party Organization in Nineteenth Century America," in *Parties and Politics in American History*, ed. L. Sandy Maisel and William G. Shade (New York: Garland, 1994), 97.

'vote' in the nineteenth century—in the parlance of the times, one 'attended' or 'went to the election.' " Casting the ballot was a matter of a few seconds, but "the election for many [male] citizens was an all-day affair devoted to greeting friends, sharing some gossip and drinks, and following the returns."[23]

Women frequently had and sometimes expressed party preferences. Reynolds' study of New Jersey found that "strong partisan feelings were inculcated at an early age in both sexes," and William Gienapp describes at least a few women who attended political meetings, joined in party celebrations, and "could not resist the attraction politics exerted even while they sometimes expressed uneasiness over their political involvement."[24] Their uneasiness was natural, because the practice of partisan politics was seen as a particularly male endeavor. The "social character of American political parties," maintains Gienapp, "froze women out of electoral politics. They simply had no more business at a polling place than they did drinking, gambling, and smoking with the boys back at the clubhouse."[25] Paula Baker argues that in their involvement with parties and electoral politics, "men could see past other differences and find common ground with other men," and that in fact the male rituals so conspicuous in late nineteenth-century electoral politics—the martial rhetoric, parades, and bonfires—gained power from their exclusion of women.[26]

America's political culture has always contained strong antiparty feelings. As Silbey notes, "partisan organizations were often viewed suspiciously even after parties had been firmly established as the basic centerpieces of American political life. A severe critique of parties, partisanship, and the activities of party organizations inten-

23. Reynolds, *Testing Democracy*, 34–35. In a study conducted by a Republican women's organization in New York in the early 1920s and discussed in chapter 3, it was found that an important obstacle to women voting was the persistence of this custom: men took the day off on election day and women were forced to stay home and tend to the farm.

24. Reynolds, *Testing Democracy*, 28; William E. Gienapp, "Politics Seems to Enter into Everything," in *Essays on Antebellum Politics, 1840–1860*, ed. S. E. Maizlish and J. J. Kushma (College Station: Texas A & M Press, 1982), 16–17.

25. Geinapp, "Politics Seems to Enter into Everything," 30.

26. Baker, *The Moral Frameworks of Public Life*, 82, and "The Domestication of Politics," 630; also see McGerr, *The Decline of Popular Politics*, and Gienapp, "Politics Seems to Enter Into Everything."

sified with the growth of independence and mugwumpery . . . from the 1870s onward."[27] The ideas of the Progressives, implemented through reforms such as nonpartisan municipal government, the Australian ballot, the direct election of senators, and personal voter registration, altered the position of the party in American politics and thus reshaped the relationship between gender and citizenship.[28] Though an extended discussion of the Progressives' ideas about parties and reform is not appropriate here, we can get a sense of some of the arguments from Charles Merriam's *The American Party System,* published in 1924. Merriam acknowledges that several theories of party have been formulated, some envisioning a positive role for the party in representative democracy, but he is quite critical of the political party as it exists in the United States. In discussing the kinds of graft and corruption that accompany the institution of a strong party machine, Merriam says: "The profits in this field of action not only cause party interest to eclipse the interest of the state, but personal and factional interests to obscure the party's interest. The spoils system originally depended upon as a means of strengthening the party, leads to the destruction of the party itself, and indeed to the paralysis of the whole party system. . . . Lines are not drawn under these conditions between parties, but follow the spoils cleavage. . . . [P]arty groups are dissolved and in their place appear the 'special interest.' . . . In this way, the advantages of the party system are largely lost."[29]

In a similar vein, Walter Lippmann wrote some years later that "the modern trouble is in a low capacity to believe in precepts which restrict and restrain private interests and desire." The public interest, on the other hand, is "what men would choose if they saw clearly, thought rationally, acted disinterestedly and benevolently."[30] In other words, Progressives, in their distaste for parties, believed that the Lockean language of liberal individualism, which

27. Silbey, "Party Organization," 100.

28. The literature on Progressivism is vast. Useful general works on the topic include Chambers, *Seedtime of Reform,* and Arthur S. Link and Richard L. McCormick, *Progressivism* (Arlington Heights IL: Harlan Davidson, 1983).

29. Charles E. Merriam, *The American Party System* (New York: Macmillan, 1924), 121.

30. Walter Lippmann, *The Public Philosophy* (Boston: Little Brown, 1955), 114, 42.

was concerned with negative freedom and individual rights, had become dominant through the parties' pursuit of private and group interests. Democracy, in their view, could be preserved only if Americans could return to the values of "civic humanism" and work toward the collective good. Thus Theodore Roosevelt "preached the republican ideals of civic authority, public duty, and even 'disinterestedness,'" and John Dewey argued that "political ideals could be sustained only through active civic participation."[31] It is hardly surprising that in this atmosphere women who were demanding suffrage (and who were often in sympathy themselves with Progressive ideas) framed their arguments in terms of women's disinterested position.

John Reynolds, in a study which examines the effects of Progressive reforms on electoral behavior in New Jersey, suggests the complex causal relationships that exist among the Progressive reforms, woman suffrage, and broader cultural changes during this era. For example, as the partisan clubs and marching companies of the nineteenth century declined, women were specifically welcomed into party gatherings. At the same time, the political techniques used by women's groups eased the movement away from campaigns of mobilization and toward campaigns of education. The change in the meaning of the vote, which had its roots in both the reforms of the electoral process and in increasing urbanization and industrialization, helped to make woman suffrage less unthinkable, while the advent of suffrage and the entry of women into electoral politics continued to forge changes in the meaning of the vote and the conception of the "good citizen."[32] The Progressive reforms had numerous consequences (unintended as well as intended), but chief among them was that they disconnected voting and elections from parties, and transformed "election day and the act of voting . . . from a partisan occasion and ritual to a civic occasion and duty."[33] This new conception of a citizen's obligations, which valued objectivity, regard for the public good, and civic participation,

31. John Patrick Diggins, "Republicanism and Progressivism," *American Quarterly* 37 (fall 1985), 575.

32. Reynolds, *Testing Democracy*, 159–64; see also Monoson, "The Lady and the Tiger," 111–13.

33. Silbey, "Party Organization," 158.

departed from the male model of citizenship that had assumed political relationships of exchange based on votes, jobs, and loyalty to friends and party. The political culture of the party period understood political virtue to be a male attribute that was tied to the expression of the inevitable passions and interests of political man. Progressive thought looked for ways to avoid or to bridge divisive private opinions in the interest of a broader public good. In encouraging the rise of experts and the reliance on scientific objectivity and empirical analysis, Progressives in effect validated the very disinterestedness that had been associated with women. "In a word, the movement from republicanism to Progressivism meant the replacement of 'virtue' by 'intelligence.'[34] Ironically, when disinterestedness and intelligence (the sort of intelligence that any good citizen could apply to a social problem) became less gendered qualities, women lost their ability to claim a unique authority as moral arbiters.[35]

"Bringing Politics Into the Home"

Paula Baker has talked about the "domestication" of politics in the late nineteenth and early twentieth centuries, describing the process by which governments took up the social responsibilities that women's activism had urged on them. We can talk about the domestication of politics in another way also: "private" women who had little experience with "larger" questions or public life were now asked to take a stand (by casting their vote) in the most public arena, on issues affecting the entire collectivity. The problems and opportunities involved in this movement into the public sphere raise the same themes that emerged in my discussion of women's citizenship in the nineteenth century: the idea that a woman's citizenship was *indirect*, through her family, and the idea that women had a special, *disinterested* view of public life. These themes emerged particularly in frequent discussions about whether women would or should make political decisions on the basis of interests they shared *as women*.

The women—suffragists, partisan activists, writers and journal-

34. Diggins, "Republicanism and Progressivism," 588.
35. See Matthews, *The Rise of Public Woman*, ch. 7, and Baker, "The Domestication of Politics," for similar arguments.

ists—who spoke and wrote about the characteristics of women's new public roles generally shared some assumptions about gender differences even as they differed on how women should exercise their expanded citizenship. Women were thought to share a range of policy goals related to their traditional concerns for children and the home. These included support of public goods such as sanitation systems, parks and recreation, and schools; legislation protecting workers, particularly women and children; and consumer protection legislation. Even at the end of the decade, Edith Nourse Rogers, a congressman from Massachusetts,[36] could write an article based on deeply held assumptions about women's distinct experiences and interests. "The American woman for generations has controlled the family pocketbook. . . . Women are bringing politics into the home. . . . In the home a woman can make a dollar go farther than a man. Now that she has the vote, she ought to be able to do the same thing for Uncle Sam's dollars. . . . Her long household training gives woman an appreciation of the need for judicious expenditures."[37]

The picture of women as having a distinctive policy agenda was sometimes overdrawn (as in the 1928 election) and was occasionally debunked, usually by party activists who pointed out that women were coming to politics from various positions in society, defined by geography, race, economics, and so forth, just as men were. Frequently such people used a universalizing theory of citizen obligation to downplay the relevance of gender differences to politics, arguing that women should now enter wholeheartedly into the male-dominated political world of parties and campaigns. For example, Felice Gordon quotes a member of the New Jersey League of Women Voters in 1926, who argued that "Perhaps we have failed to recognize fully that when we were enfranchised . . . our own status and therefore our own obligations were definitely changed. No longer outside the government . . . we were now inside and therefore obligated to assume the responsibility and to

36. It should be noted that "congressman," "chairman," and the like were the commonly used terms, by both women and men, when women occupied those offices.

37. Edith Nourse Rogers, "Women's New Place in Politics," *Nation's Business* 18 (August 1930), 39–41, 120, 124.

perform the full duties of citizenship through the regularly estab-lished governmental channels."[38] Similarly, Ruth Hanna McCor-mick, a member of Congress during the 1920s, said of women that "we are not 100% American Citizens until we discharge our duties to government as faithfully as we discharge our duties to the home."[39] In this view, suffrage asserted woman's individuality and self-interest, as opposed to submerging her interests in those of the family. This was true even when many of the arguments for suffrage were based on justifications of expediency; regardless of the arguments that were used to support granting women suffrage, the vote itself was clearly an *individual* right. Thus the anti-suffragists were right to fear the effects of the Nineteenth Amend-ment—not because it increased the divorce rate, overburdened women, or unsexed them, but because having the right to vote was an individual right that challenged the long-standing view of women's citizenship as *indirect,* mediated by husband and family.[40] The ongoing discussion about whether women's citizenship would take a distinct form illustrates one way that the difference-equality dilemma was played out, revealing a tension between advocacy of a "maternalist" political agenda and the realization that such an agenda was based on women's confinement to the private realm.

That women could now participate in the public arena through the vote did not change the average woman's absorption in her domestic interests and responsibilities. Suffragists and party activ-ists alike worried about this problem, and the League of Women Voters had an explicit goal to transform women from private to public individuals. The League discovered early in its existence that they couldn't simply "get out the vote" but needed to give people reasons to vote. A connection needed to be made between people's private experience and public affairs. This was particularly necessary for women, who were "still engrossed in personal and family problems and interests. The League has discovered that this

38. Felice Gordon, "After Winning: The New Jersey Suffragists, 1910–1947" (Ph.D. thesis, Rutgers University, 1982), 137.

39. Kristie Miller, *Ruth Hanna McCormick: A Life in Politics 1880–1944* (Albu-querque: University of New Mexico Press, 1992), 159.

40. Degler, *At Odds,* ch. 14; DuBois, *Feminism and Suffrage;* and see Carole Pateman, "Woman, Nature, and the Suffrage," *Ethics* 90 (July 1980).

is the real starting point of sound political education. Orienting activities need to center in food or school or playgrounds or electric rates or taxes—not just any one of these but in that particular one which is at the moment a matter of concern to the particular woman whose interest is to be attached to government."[41]

In the views of the early leaders of the League, this kind of educational work, which made clear the connections between the (traditionally defined) private and public spheres, was just as important as legislative lobbying. The League attempted to activate the connections between private and public in two ways: by making clear the connections between public policy and individual lives (as discussed above), and by stressing the cooperative nature of democracy.[42] The League of Women Voters and other women's organizations consciously acted to extend women's traditional, private, and domestic roles into the public realm by providing opportunities for women to deliberate on public issues and to take or support actions relevant to those issues.[43]

Whether a woman's point of view was indeed a disinterested one was also a subject of discussion during this period. It was widely accepted that women's participation in politics sprang from different motivations than men's. In this view, women were coming to the *polis* from the private sphere, where they were concerned with health, order, and the future, because of their central involvement with children and with caring for their homes and families. Thus they would vote and participate in politics from a disinterested, altruistic perspective. Clearly many suffragists framed expediency arguments with the idea that women were better than men, and certainly more compassionate and moral. Women who took this position argued that women, as citizens, should set themselves apart from men, though of course they should vote. Their "prime

41. Sara B. Brumbaugh, "Democratic Experience and Education in the League of Women Voters" (Ph.D. thesis, Columbia University, 1946), 49.

42. The League's vision is similar to what Benjamin Barber has called "strong democracy." See Barber's *Strong Democracy* (Berkeley: University of California Press, 1984).

43. See Naomi Black, *Social Feminism* (Ithaca: Cornell University Press, 1989); Brumbaugh, *Democratic Experience and Education;* and Louise Young, *In the Public Interest: The League of Women Voters, 1920–1970* (New York: Greenwood Press, 1989).

role would be to serve as a moral force, essentially outside the political structure, though not disassociated from it. Women would act as prodders to remind those within the system what course they must properly pursue."[44] Mary Anderson, the Director of the Women's Bureau in the 1920s, thought that "women's organizations operated from motives and resources different from those of men's chambers of commerce, fraternal organizations, manufacturers' associations and so on. Where men's pressure groups relied on economic power in politics and looked for commercial or financial advantage or professional gain, women's organizations were working without self-interest, for the public good, for social welfare. . . ."[45]

Moreover, as Elisabeth Israels Perry argues in her biography of Belle Moskowitz, "the few models of successful political women available . . . in the 1920s were women involved in politics less for the purpose of advancing their own careers than to promote ideals and programs." Moskowitz herself played an extremely important role in formulating Al Smith's policies as governor and in running his gubernatorial and presidential campaigns; but she did so "from the sidelines, plying her knitting needles and speaking only when asked for her views."[46]

Other women saw *all* citizens, male and female, as having the potential to be "good citizens" in the sense of ceding primacy to the public interest. While women were seen as ideal citizens from a Progressive point of view—they were less swayed by party appeals, more willing to consider the merits of arguments—this difference was only historical. Those who created the League of Women Voters, for example, did so on the basis of an extremely

44. Felice Gordon, *After Winning: The Legacy of the New Jersey Suffragists, 1920–1947* (New Brunswick: Rutgers University Press, 1986), 53. Of course such "social prodding" could be done without any involvement in the electoral system, as many of the anti-suffragists pointed out. Thomas Jablonsky argues that many of the anti-suffragists were also social feminists, but though they addressed similar problems, they believed women's obligations should be carried out through the molding of public opinion to support progressive laws. See Thomas J. Jablonsky, *Duty, Nature and Stability: The Female Anti-Suffragists in the United States, 1894–1920* (Ph.D. thesis, University of California at Los Angeles, 1978), 227–36.

45. Cott, *The Grounding of Modern Feminism*, 99.

46. Elisabeth Israels Perry, *Belle Moskowitz* (New York: Oxford University Press, 1987), xi and 153.

positive view of human capabilities and motives, not simply from the conviction that *women* were uniquely unselfish. Belle Sherwin, the second president of the national League, said in 1927: "The League depends upon discussions—upon the exchange of ideas and experience . . . to get at the facts of situations, seeking political wisdom. So gradually, . . . there is developed among us a wider and deeper understanding of the situations in which we find ourselves; a setting for situations, as it were, which helps to account for them, making clearer what government can rightly do and what it cannot; what expectations we may entertain of it for the good life of all the people."[47] Robert Fowler, in his biography of Carrie Chapman Catt, argues that she did not think, or claim, that women were "purer or nobler than men," but that they were free of the "history, culture, and current practice of modern politics" and thus their values were better.[48] Of course this position usually left unresolved the question of whether women's values would change once they became deeply involved in the "current practice of modern politics."

Finally, women (and men) argued during this period about whether their political styles, the way they accomplished things in the public arena, were basically different. Women activists and political observers generally perceived male and female political styles as being at odds. Emily Newell Blair wrote an article in 1926 called "Men in Politics as a Woman Sees Them." She had come to the conclusion that men accomplished things primarily though *competition* with one another, women through what she called the "program method" (cooperating under definite rules of procedure to solve a problem). She gave an example of a state where women wanted to organize for their party (Democratic) in order to educate and mobilize voters before the primary. The men protested, sure that this really represented work for one or the other of the primary candidates. "Every political organization is to men a battleground and they cannot understand a club in which women will work for a program regardless of candidates," said Blair. To women, men in politics "look like gladiators. We find them fighting animals. And

47. Quoted in Brumbaugh, *Democratic Experience and Education*, 25.
48. Robert Booth Fowler, *Carrie Catt: Feminist Politician* (Boston: Northeastern University Press, 1986), 66.

we find their organization based on competition, on the contest method."[49] On the other hand, some women criticized the more refined methods of their own sex. Emily Newell Blair's sister, Margaretta Newell, wrote in 1930 that women were too diffident, trusting, modest, polite, and pacifistic to get anywhere in a political fight. They are reluctant to recognize that practical politics involves conflict. She urged women to "start fights," get publicity, gain followers, and take risks.[50]

THE LADY AND THE TIGER: WOMEN'S THINKING ABOUT PARTY POLITICS

The change toward a somewhat less gendered notion of citizenship may have been underway during the last years of the suffrage movement, but the writings and speeches of the suffragists show that the civic norms of what has been called "the party period" still had a powerful hold on them. Though women's groups had pioneered in the development of lobbying and other non-electoral political tactics, virtually all of the suffragists saw the major parties as the locus of political power. For example, in 1909 one woman observer of the suffrage movement issued this warning about the inflated expectations surrounding the question of woman suffrage "Disillusionment only can result from the claim that women when enfranchised will at once right wrongs, however deep-seated they may be in the body politic, and abolish corruption, though it is intrenched in an established, complicated system, and practised by astute and experienced men in the interest of their own personal profit; for such a claim is, in its nature, unreasonable, and doomed to disappointment."[51] And when Carrie Chapman Catt spoke to the February 1920 convention, which was the last meeting of the National American Woman Suffrage Association and the first of the National League of Women Voters, she described the empirical reality of powerful political parties: "It is not a question of

49. Emily Newell Blair, "Men in Politics as a Woman Sees Them," *Harpers Magazine* 152 (May 1926), 703–9.

50. Margaretta Newell, "Must Women Fight in Politics?" *Woman's Journal,* January 1930, 10–11, 34–35.

51. Helen Thomas Flexner, "Introduction," in *Equal Suffrage* by Helen L. Sumner (New York: Harper & Brothers, 1909), xviii–xvix.

whether they ought to be powerful or ought not to be powerful; they are."[52]

Parties were the linchpins of power and change, and it is important to realize also that parties *were* politics in the 1920s, in the eyes of many men and women. It is easy for us today to conceive of a person being "politically active" in, say, an environmental organization, or a neighborhood group demanding more police protection, without having any strong party affiliation. In the 1920s, however, the connection between parties and politics was much closer.

Because parties were central to concepts of politics, and because women were historically ambivalent toward parties, much of the discussion about how women would use suffrage focused on how they would deal with the political parties.[53] Should women participate in politics mainly through the traditional avenues (i.e., the parties) or from some new, nonpartisan or apartisan stance? In Connecticut, for example, as in other states, suffragists debated the question of joining the parties and taking positions within parties: whether to attempt reform from inside the parties or "hold a position as independent voters and reform from outside."[54]

Over many years, a consistent strain of thought among suffragists had envisioned and endorsed active participation in party politics by voting women. Elizabeth Cady Stanton had argued that women, once they had the vote, *must* be involved with the parties "inasmuch as our demands are to be made and carried, like other political questions, by the aid of and affiliation with parties."[55] In 1912 Jane Addams, from her highly visible position in the new Progressive party, had argued that the time had come for women to become active in the parties. She worked to explain not only why

52. *Woman Citizen,* 28 February 1920.

53. Melanie Gustafson's recent research shows that this discussion had been going on at least since 1912, with respect to women's role in partisan and electoral politics. Melanie Gustafson, "The Women of 1912: The Struggle for Inclusion in the Political Parties," paper presented at the Organization of American Historians meetings, Atlanta, GA (April 1994).

54. Nichols, *Votes and More for Women,* 38.

55. Elizabeth Cady Stanton, unpublished manuscript, "What Should Be Our Attitude toward Parties?" excerpted in Elizabeth Cady Stanton and Susan B. Anthony, *Correspondence, Writings, Speeches,* ed. Ellen Carol DuBois (New York: Shocken Books, 1981), 182.

women should support the Progressive party but also "why women should engage in party work and why partisanship was an acceptable political identity for women."[56] Addams argued that the only way that women could have the policy impact they desired was to work through the parties. Catt's recommendations that the members of the National American Woman Suffrage Association enter the parties was based on her perception that parties dominated the political process. Given this, she said, the only stance from which women could accomplish what they wanted was inside the party. In fact, it was unimaginable to her that women might "continue on the outside of those political parties where we have been for sixty years and to go on appealing for their favor as we have always been doing. Are we going to petition them as we have always done? Well, if so, what was the use of getting the vote?"[57] She admitted that the parties needed reform, but acknowledged that they were an essential part of the democratic process within which women should work. Like other women loyal to a party, Emily Newell Blair, a Democrat who was eventually elected vice chairman of the party and who in 1921 convinced the party to elect rather than appoint committeewomen, argued that there were only two ways for women to get political power: by holding office and by becoming effective in political organizations.[58] Similar pleas at the beginning of the decade were made by partisans such as Mary Garrett Hay and Harriet Taylor Upton, all of whom were straightforward in their acceptance of the partisan structuring of politics, the inevitability of parties, and the necessity for women to work through the parties.

When Ruth McCormick spoke to the national convention of the League of Women Voters in November 1924, she "created a

56. Gustafson, "The Women of 1912," 15.

57. Carrie Chapman Catt, "Political Parties and Women Voters" (address delivered to the Congress of the League of Women Voters, Chicago, 14 February 1920). Women's Rights Collection, Box 56, F747, Schlesinger Library.

58. Margot Jerrard, "Emily Newell Blair," in *Notable American Women: The Modern Period,* ed. Barbara Sicherman (Cambridge: Harvard University Press, 1980). It is interesting to note that by the end of the decade Blair was quite disillusioned. She said publicly that male party officials had not and probably would not accept women, and advocated separate women's political organizations, working primarily for women candidates. See chapter 4.

sensation" when she announced "I do not like the League." She advised women to quit the League and join a party. "This government is a party government," she went on. "I have been taken to task for criticizing the League. I am not criticizing the League. It has its functions. Those functions are educational. . . . The League may start you off, but you cannot continue [your work] by reclining in the League . . . you have to join a good party."[59] Theodora Youmans, a Wisconsin Republican, reminded other women that she did not "abdicate my mind and conscience by joining a party. I make my mind and conscience effective by joining the minds and consciences of others and so acquiring weight and influence."[60] Frances Perkins, a reformer who came to see the benefits of working with Tammany Hall, took a similar position. Like many other women activists, she accepted the notion that for the most part, political power resided in the parties. Unlike some, however, she saw that this kind of power could provide her with the resources necessary to accomplish her policy goals. In addition, she came to see choosing a party and sticking with it as a pragmatic judgment call; in effect one picked the party that demonstrated the greatest likelihood of success in producing one's preferred policies. Men such as Al Smith and Robert Wagner valued party loyalty and regularity for good reason, she concluded: "it is the basis of the two-party system."[61]

Other women, however, accepted the Progressive critique of parties, believing that parties by definition produced self-interested politics and, at least in the American context, produced corrupt politics as well. One of the most impassioned arguments of this type was that of Winifred Starr Dobyns, the first chairman of the Republican Women's Committee of Illinois. In an article entitled "The Lady and the Tiger (Or, the Woman Voter and the Political Machine)," she wrote, "Let us be frank. With some possible excep-

59. Miller, *Ruth Hanna McCormick*, 159.

60. *Woman Citizen*, 24 February 1920: 841.

61. Winifred Wandersee, "Frances Perkins Meets Tammany Hall: The Co-Adaptation of Machine Politics and Social Reform, 1910–1918" (paper presented at the Conference on Women, Politics and Change, New School for Social Research, New York, NY, April 1990).

tions, the aim of the political organizations is not good government, patriotic service, public welfare. These are but phrases used for campaign purposes. Political organizations are, for the most part, designed to fill the pockets of politicians at public expense, to give jobs to thousands who find politics an easy way to make a living, to maintain men in office who can do favors for business." Dobyns went on to recommend that women act to change parties *as voters.* Parties cannot be changed through the regular party organizations, she argued, but the quality of candidates would improve if people vote in party primaries for reform candidates. The idea of reforming "from within," she argued, "is a delusion. To join it means to condone its actions, to accept its standards. This is not the way to carry on the fight for decency."[62]

Dobyns and others commented on women's status as outsiders and reformers in party politics. For the most part women were seen and saw themselves in the 1920s as less partisan than men. An understanding of the gender distinctions in nineteenth- and early twentieth-century public life, as well as what we know about how individuals develop a party identification, would lead us to expect that the newly enfranchised women would be less enthusiastic partisans. In his study of Illinois, where men's and women's ballots were kept separate from 1913 to 1921, Joel Goldstein found that women were less "dedicated" to the parties: they were less likely to vote in primaries or uncontested elections and evidenced a higher rate of ticket splitting than men.[63] Felice Gordon, in her account of the political activities of New Jersey suffragists in the 1920s, describes the disputes within the parties that occurred because even those women who did become active in the parties tended to be a bit more independent-minded than the parties were used to. In a move similar to Dobyns, Mary Garrett Hay of New York resigned the vice chairmanship of the state party when it supported the re-election of James Wadsworth, an opponent of

62. Winifred Starr Dobyns, "The Lady and the Tiger," *Woman Citizen,* January 1927, 45.

63. Joel H. Goldstein, "The Effects of the Adoption of Woman Suffrage: Sex Differences in Voting Behavior—Illinois, 1914–1921" (Ph.D. thesis, University of Chicago, 1973).

suffrage; in fact she helped organize an anti-Wadsworth committee.[64] This stance, which might be termed "independent partisanship," was assumed by many suffragists who preferred one party
over the other but believed that loyalty to a party should be contin-
gent on the positions it took and the candidates it offered.

If committed partisanship and independent partisanship were
two of the possible ways that women might exercise their new
citizenship rights, nonpartisanship constituted a third. Paula Baker
describes the nonpartisanship of rural New York women: "By re-
fusing to identify with any party, women could pick and choose
among the candidates on the basis of their positions on issues and
personal moral standing." Nonpartisanship also fit with a broader
conception of how politics worked—a "civics textbook" view that
"idealized the independent, public-spirited citizen of the civics
books, not the partisan. It was a rational rather than an emotional
ideal: intelligence, attention to the public good, and Christian values were the attributes of dutiful citizens and legislators." Some
of these rural New York women did affiliate with parties, of course,
but these women's partisan groups still took a "rational" approach
to politics. "While partisan, these women believed that their connections to the Republican Party grew out of their careful consideration of issues and the positions of the parties. The Republican
women's loyalty rested on a different foundation from that of the
men."[65]

In many ways, the League of Women Voters, the successor organization to the National American Woman Suffrage Association,
followed this nonpartisan ideal. The League was formed to educate
women, and all citizens, to formulate positions on policy and to
participate intelligently in politics. Its founders referred to the
League as nonpartisan, "unpartisan," or (on at least one occasion)
"pan-partisan." This was despite the fact that the League encouraged its members to become involved with party politics, a position
based on Catt's belief that corrupt as the parties might be, "it is
vain to try to get hold of the steering wheel until you get into the
boat."[66] It was recognized, of course, that individual women might

64. Gordon, *After Winning*, 87; Young, *In the Public Interest*, 47.
65. Baker, *The Moral Frameworks of Public Life*, 82–85.
66. *Woman Citizen*, 28 February 1920.

have difficulty deciding how to allocate time and energy between party work and League work, and even that those women who became too involved in party work might not be able to continue to work in the nonpartisan League.[67]

Organizationally, nonpartisanship meant that the League refrained from endorsing candidates. This stemmed in part from a fear that partisan involvement would embroil the League in petty local quarrels, but more importantly this policy represented a crucial aspect of the League's political stance.[68] An interesting clarification of this stance (and illustration of the confusion that sometimes accompanied it) appears in a letter from Carrie Chapman Catt to Edna Fishel Gelhorn in 1920: "In my effort to make clear that we do not intend to be a third party or to oppose women going into the regular parties, I probably have expressed myself very lamely. Of course the League of Women Voters in New York is against Wadsworth [a notorious anti-suffragist] and had so announced itself before St. Louis. I do not think we can make a rule that no candidates are to be worked against, but what I was trying to make clear was that we are not going to endorse candidates as between the parties."[69]

The League's commitment to nonpartisanship produced tensions; it was misunderstood by many politicians, most notably New York's governor Nathan Miller, who addressed a New York League convention in 1921 by saying that the two-party system was so essential to democracy that any non-party political organization was a "menace to our free institutions and to representative government."[70] Although New York editorial writers immediately accused Miller of being motivated primarily by his opposition to the League's welfare program, he accurately perceived the ideas of many of the LWV founders and other former suffragists (even those who worked within the parties) as constituting a strong critique, if not an outright rejection, of the party system.

67. Louise Young, in her recent study of the League of Women Voters, describes the difficulties that the League experienced in reconciling nonpartisanship with party activity by its members and leaders. Young, *In the Public Interest*, 94.

68. Fowler, *Carrie Catt*, 102.

69. Catt to Gelhorn, Gelhorn Papers, box 1, folder 7, Schlesinger Library.

70. Cott, *The Grounding of Modern Feminism*, 106–9; Carrie Chapman Catt, "A Teapot in a Tempest," *Woman Citizen*, 5 February 1921.

When activist women discussed the political opportunities opening up for women in the 1920s, they shared assumptions about the way women interacted with others and solved problems and about women's common political agenda. They also assumed that most women shared an antipathy to the kind of personal ambition and political friendship (involving favors and bargaining and party loyalty) that characterized male politics. Thus women who sought to advance their ideas about social and political change within what they perceived as a system still dominated by parties were faced with a dilemma: how to alter what had been a very clear boundary between male and female styles and practices while maintaining the virtues they saw as inherent in their own history. As Emily Newell Blair put it, "Whether politics will make women into a fighting animal or whether women will make politics into a club— that remains to be seen."[71] Of course at the same time that women were developing their approach to party and electoral politics, their work in women's and reform groups both before and after suffrage refined, popularized, and legitimized a new kind of interest group politics, based on information and education, and thus contributed to the decline of party-based politics.[72]

The major part of the debate about parties and partisanship was carried out at the level of elites: should well-educated, active women leaders try to work through parties or independently of parties? If they were to be involved in the parties, should they give unconditional loyalty as the parties demanded, or should they withhold support until their own demands were answered? Should women form separate women's organizations within the parties or support groups outside the official parties?[73] But this debate among the elite had implications for mass politics as well, both because the arguments made by each side were accessible to all women

71. Blair, "Men in Politics as a Woman Sees Them," 709.
72. This is an argument supported in part by the work of Elisabeth Clemens ("Organizational Repertoires and Institutional Change"), which I discuss more fully in chapter 6.
73. For an account of this debate in New Jersey, see Gordon, *After Winning*. Nichols, in *Votes and More for Women*, describes similar arguments that were used in Connecticut in the 1920s.

voters (through publications such as the *Woman Citizen, Ladies Home Journal,* and others), and because the position taken by elites in a particular locale could have an important effect on the level and direction of the mobilization of female voters. The next chapter examines variations and trends in women's registration and voting over the decade of the 1920s.

"Who Gets the Cake?"
(From *Literary Digest*, August 7, 1920, p. 21.)

THREE   Women as Voters

*First in interest, if not in performance, is the question of vot-
ing. Having secured the right, do they exercise that right? If
not universally, do they exercise it with increasing or decreasing
interest? With increasing or declining effectiveness?*

Sophonisba Breckinridge, *Women in the Twentieth Century*, 1933.

As the last chapter makes clear, the contours of the changes
in the voting universe that would be ushered in by the
Nineteenth Amendment were the subject of speculation
and contention. In writing about the advent of woman suffrage in
1920, historians and political scientists have often looked at electoral behavior in the 1920s through lenses colored by the debates
and predictions surrounding the suffrage amendment. In particular, it is often assumed that the right to vote in all elections was
automatically conferred with the amendment's ratification in August 1920, and that women's failure to take advantage of their new
right accounts for the extremely low voter turnout recorded in the
1920s. But the boundary that created a gendered political arena
in which men voted and women did not was not quickly or easily erased, even after Tennessee finally ratified the Nineteenth
Amendment, the thirty-sixth state to do so. This chapter discusses
the male political establishment's persisting resistance to shifting
this boundary and the reasons for the great variation in the extent
to which women became involved in electoral politics during the
decade of the twenties. Looking for relationships between social
characteristics and political involvement provides part of the picture; understanding the radical cultural changes involved in re-
conceiving electoral politics as a no longer exclusively male domain
provides another part. Equally important is placing the electoral
behavior of women into a specific political context. This perspective instructs us to look for explanations for declining turnout that

take into account the general politics of the twenties rather than focusing exclusively on women, and it also tells us that whether women in particular localities registered or voted in particular years was heavily dependent on the mobilizing activities of local party (and other) organizations.

CHANGE AND RESISTANCE

By the time the suffrage amendment was ratified in 1920, fifteen states had already given women full suffrage (a total of over 7,300,000 eligible women voters) and twelve others had legislated suffrage in presidential elections (most of the latter in 1919).[1] For those women who were given voting rights by the amendment, the ability to vote for all offices was not automatically conferred on August 26, 1920. Each state had to change its laws, sometimes by convening special sessions of its legislature; and states and counties had to undertake the work of registering women, sometimes by means of special dispensations so that they could vote in the 1920 elections. In fact, women in Mississippi and Georgia did not vote in the November elections, since authorities there upheld the laws requiring four month's residence prior to an election.

Other problems and legal questions abounded. Could lists of women registered to vote in school elections (which was allowed in many states) be used as registration lists for state and national elections? Could women vote for delegates to the national conventions? The Wisconsin Attorney General said no to the latter question; his Nebraska counterpart said yes. The Kansas City Commissioner of Elections ruled that women voters who married following their registration could not vote: changing their name on marriage meant that they "cease to exist as registered voters."[2] In Tampa, on the other hand, women had been assured by city officials "that they need not hurry to register, and that the books would be brought to them in their homes." This was not true, of course, and

1. States that granted full suffrage were Arizona, California, Colorado, Idaho, Kansas, Michigan, Montana, Nevada, New York, Oklahoma, Oregon, South Dakota, Utah, Washington, and Wyoming. States that granted suffrage for presidential elections were Illinois, Indiana, Iowa, Maine, Minnesota, Missouri, Nebraska, North Dakota, Ohio, Rhode Island, Tennessee, and Wisconsin. Illinois, Nebraska, North Dakota and Tennessee had also granted municipal suffrage.

2. *Woman Citizen*, 1 November 1920, 665.

women who investigated found that the registration books would close in four days.[3] In Chicago, the Election Commissioner ruled that women "could not be barred from registering on the grounds that they were not self-supporting," as some suffrage opponents had suggested.[4]

Thus certainly in the 1920 elections, and extending in some cases to later elections, women's ability to register and to vote was not a given but was a subject of negotiation. In addition, strong assumptions about women's domestic responsibilities often constrained their ability to register, vote, or otherwise participate in electoral politics. When women registered to vote in New York City in 1920, it was reported that "In some districts, fifty and sixty baby carriages were grouped outside of a polling place at the same time," a reminder that while women were taking on a new public role, they retained all their private obligations as well.[5] A study of voting in the 1922 election conducted by Republican women in New York, though it discovered some high female turnout in rural areas, also found that in general turnout was lower in areas where conditions were harder and farms more isolated. In some places, tradition dictated that men took a day off on election day, drove to the polling place, and stayed until dark talking politics. The women were forced to stay home on the farm and thus had no chance to vote even if they wanted to.[6]

Nor did all women who could legally vote in 1920, or later in the decade, choose to do so. Some opponents of suffrage had predicted that women might register, but would be discouraged from participating in such an archetypally male act as voting. There were also hyperbolic predictions, on the part of both suffragists and anti-suffragists, of an outpouring of female votes, enough to double the electorate. But the number of votes cast in the 1920 election was only a 30% increase from 1916; in other words, the percentage of eligible voters who went to the polls declined over those four years. The coincidence of the record low voting turnouts

3. *Woman Citizen,* 3 October 1920, 603.

4. *New York Times,* 14 October 1920 (III), 2.

5. *New York Times,* 10 October 1920, 5.

6. Sarah Schuyler Butler, "Women Who Do Not Vote," *Scribner's Magazine* 76 (November 1924), 532.

of the twenties with the advent of women's suffrage has made it easy for political scientists and historians to assume that women's suffrage accounted for the decline in turnout. This hypothesis implies further (in the absence of data that allow separate analysis of male and female voting) that turnout among women was quite low; that many (if not most) women who received the vote did not make use of it. As I argued in chapter 1, situating the turnout levels of the 1920s in the proper historical and political context supports Burnham's contention that "there is less than meets the eye in this famous woman-suffrage variable."[7]

Modern survey research was not yet widely used in the 1920s, and it is difficult (sometimes impossible) to untangle women's political behavior from men's using aggregate data such as vote totals and registration data. In 1937, Herbert Tingsten wrote that "there exists no wholly complete and reliable material" with which to examine male and female voting patterns in the United States. Unlike European countries, such statistics are not kept at a national level, and states have very different reporting customs. If we are interested in the rate at which American women were integrated into the political system (i.e., became voters), it is unfortunate but true that the data which could be used to form a definitive picture do not exist. Only Illinois kept men's and women's ballots separate, and only for a few years, from 1913 to 1921.[8] Many states had no registration requirements, or required registration only in cities, during this period. A few states (such as Oregon) and some cities did keep separate registration statistics for men and women for certain time periods, and some detailed work, discussed later in this chapter, has been done that looks at registration lists in city wards and precincts.[9]

7. Burnham, "Theory and Voting Research," 1015; Kleppner, "Were Women to Blame?"

8. The most extensive analysis of the Illinois voting data is Goldstein, *The Effects of the Adoption of Woman Suffrage.*

9. Gerald Gamm, *The Making of New Deal Democrats: Voting Behavior and Realignment in Boston, 1920–1940* (Chicago: University of Chicago Press, 1986); David Burner, *The Politics of Provincialism: The Democratic Party in Transition, 1918–1932* (New York: W. W. Norton, 1967), 68–70, 229–30; see also Samuel Lubbell, *The Future of American Politics* (New York: Harper, 1951), 40; William Claggett and John Van Wingen, "Conversion and Recruitment in Boston during the New Deal Realignment: A Preliminary Comparison of Men and Women,"

The failure of some of the early studies to produce an accurate picture of women's political behavior in part simply reflects these data problems. In one of the earliest attempts to examine women's voting, William Ogburn and Inez Goltra studied voters in Portland, Oregon in 1914. They concluded, rather surprisingly, that women voters were less likely than men to support Progressive reforms (included on the ballot were referenda on protective labor legislation, state aid to the unemployed, proportional representation, and primary elections for selection of convention delegates), but their study relied simply on a correlation between the vote and the percentage of women in the electorate—a clear example of the ecological fallacy.[10] Other early studies by Rice and Willey focused on estimating the overall turnout of Northern women, but lack of separate statistics for men and women forced them to rely on assumptions (e.g., that male voting turnout had declined at an identical rate during the last twenty years of the nineteenth century and during 1900 to 1920) which we now know to be incorrect.[11] It is also the case that studies conducted during this period (like later ones) rested on gender-specific assumptions. Nancy Cott points out that Merriam and Gosnell's *Non-Voting*, published in 1924 and most influential in framing public thinking about women's political participation, "tended to dismiss rather than encourage women as voters; in fact it portrayed women as characteristic nonvoters."[12]

Clearly, women's turnout, as far as we can ascertain, was lower than men's during this decade. This is what we would expect from any newly enfranchised group. Just as clearly, however, the 1920s represent a period of dealignment, characterized by low turnout and decreasing party loyalties, and women's political behavior, like men's, reflected this. The remainder of this chapter focuses on the

paper presented at the Southern Political Science Association meetings, Atlanta, November 1990; Kristi Andersen, "Women and the Vote in the 1920s: What Happened in Oregon," *Women and Politics* 14 (1994), 43–56.

10. Ogburn and Goltra, "How Women Vote."

11. Rice and Willey, "American Women's Ineffective Use of the Vote;" Stuart D. Rice and Malcolm M. Willey, "A Sex Cleavage in the Presidential Election of 1920," *Journal of the American Statistical Association* 19 (1924), 519–20. See Burnham, "The Changing Shape of the American Political Universe," for evidence on declining turnout.

12. Cott, *The Grounding of Modern Feminism*, 104.

more interesting and less often asked questions about variations in the extent to which women apparently voted and the rates at which women as voters became incorporated into the electorate.

VARIATIONS IN WOMEN'S VOTING RATES

If we reexamine the contemporary accounts, including journalistic descriptions of the "woman vote," along with more recent, methodologically sophisticated studies, we can begin to understand the variability in the rate at which women voted in the 1920s. One is struck, in the newspaper accounts of elections in the 1920s and in the available voting and registration data, by the large differences in the levels at which women in different states, counties, cities, and towns turned out to vote. The boundaries delineating women's proper behaviors with regard to politics clearly changed much more quickly in some areas than in others, and it is equally true that well into the 1950s and the era of reliable survey data, there was a consistent tendency for women, particularly older women, to be less involved in politics and to vote less frequently than men. A careful look at the data that are available can help to explain why this particular boundary seemed easier to shift in some contexts than in others.

Examples of variability in voting rates include a study, conducted by the Republican Women's State Executive Committee of New York, of voting in the 1922 mid-year elections. In one county, the ratio of female to male voters was .95; in four others, it ranged from .88 to .93. All these were rural and, with one exception, Republican. On the other hand, the county with the smallest ratio of female to male voters (.39) was also rural and Republican. In the boroughs of New York City, ratios ranged from .57 to .69. In a sample of Illinois counties, the ratio of women to men voting for President in 1916 varied from a low of .44 to a high of .78.[13]

Voter registration figures for Chicago wards in 1920 are similarly varied. Some wards, mostly in areas with predominantly native-born populations, showed women's registration (as a percentage of adults) at nearly 50%, while two wards in which nearly half the male adult population were foreign-born had female registration

13. New York figures are from Butler, "Women Who Do Not Vote," 529–30. Illinois data are from Illinois Blue Book 1917–1919, 582–84.

levels of about 20%. The male-female difference among wards (based on the percentage of adults registered) ranged from 15 to 33 percentage points.[14] Deriving a ratio (the ratio of the percent of eligible females registered to the percent of eligible males registered) allows us to compare these figures with the statewide and New York figures above. These figures range from .49 (for the Nineteenth Ward, a near–West Side, poor, Italian area) to .70 (for the Seventh Ward, which included Hyde Park and the University of Chicago). Helen Sumner, in an earlier and exhaustive survey-based study of women's political involvement in Colorado, had also found great variation. As one example, the percentage difference between men and women registrants in 1906 was only 2.3% in the city of Boulder, but 22% in the rural county of La Plata.[15] We can thus agree with the New York Republican women, who concluded "that the proportion of women who vote depends upon local conditions, rather than any general causes."[16]

What are the "local conditions" that could explain such variation? One factor that might have inhibited women's voting, particularly in the years immediately following the ratification of the Nineteenth Amendment, is simply the persistence of anti-suffrage attitudes. Merriam and Gosnell found in their study of Chicago that 13% of the women nonvoters they interviewed cited "disbelief in women's voting" or "objections of husband to women voting" as the primary cause of their failure to register or vote. One out of every nine women nonvoters interviewed admitted that she had not adjusted herself yet to the idea of women voting. The strength of this disbelief varied from an attitude of mild indifference toward women's civic responsibilities to a "confirmed conviction that women should keep out of politics altogether. . . . [Some of] the disgusted anti-suffragists adopted somewhat of a superior attitude toward "the dirty game of politics that the men are wont to play."[17] Jablonsky, in his study of anti-suffragists, also claims that while some became "conscientious members of the voting public," others

14. Goldstein, *The Effects of the Adoption of Woman Suffrage*, 89–93.

15. Helen Sumner, *Equal Suffrage* (New York: Harper & Brothers, 1909), 25–29, 103.

16. Butler, "Women Who Do Not Vote."

17. Merriam and Gosnell, *Non-Voting*, 109–10.

"continued to believe that politics were for men . . . despite their technical enfranchisement." It was found in New York in the mid-1920s that "in every town" there were "some anti-suffrage women who refuse[d] to take any part in politics."[18]

On the other hand, there is evidence that in some places even leading anti-suffragists voted and urged other women to vote. For example, in North Carolina, "though never a suffragist, Mrs. Bickett [the governor's wife] appealed to the women of the state to register and vote. May Hilliard Hinton, president of the North Carolina branch of the Rejection League [an anti-suffrage organization], made a similar appeal."[19] In a *New York Times* article in 1928, a woman campaign worker was described (possibly with some exaggeration) as likely to be "a lady completely forgetful that she once crusaded to keep women safe in the home. There are no anti-suffragists now."[20]

Table 3.1 indicates that at high levels of aggregation, in both states and cities, there is a rough correspondence between the level of women's participation and the year their state adopted suffrage. Oregon and California, Western states where women had suffrage well before 1920, show the highest percentage of eligible women registered to vote. In Los Angeles, where women received suffrage in 1911, and Oregon, which approved suffrage in 1912, over 50% of women over twenty-one (almost 65% in Oregon) were registered, while in Illinois, Rhode Island, and Vermont less than half the eligible women were registered, a figure that drops to 33% for white women in Louisiana. In general, the southern states were less sympathetic to woman suffrage than the North; Breckinridge points out that in 1924, women constituted only 28% of the registered voters in Louisiana, while they were 42% in Pennsylvania and 44% in Rhode Island.[21] At a lower level of analysis, the hypothesis that pro-suffrage sentiment would lead to higher participation

18. Jablonsky, *Duty, Nature and Stability,* 139; "Butler, Women Who Do Not Vote," 533.

19. A. Elizabeth Taylor, "The Woman Suffrage Movement in North Carolina," *North Carolina Historical Review* 38 (January and April, 1961), 189.

20. Anne O'Hare McCormick, "Enter Women, the New Boss of Politics," *New York Times Magazine,* 21 October 1928, 3.

21. Sophonisba P. Breckinridge, *Women in the Twentieth Century* (New York: McGraw-Hill, 1933), 250–51.

3.1 Woman Suffrage and Women's Registration in the 1920s

State	Year suffrage granted	Year data compiled	Women (percent of voters registered)	Men (percent of voters registered)	Female to male ratio	Source
California (L.A.)	1911	1930	53.0	57.9	.91	SB 249–50 & 1930 Census
Oregon	1912	1924	64.6	84.9	.76	Blue Book & 1920 Census
Illinois (Chicago)	1912/1920°	1924	49.0	74.9	.66	SB 249
Rhode Island	1917	1924	44.1	55.9	.79	SB 251
Pennsylvania	1920°	1925	41.8	58.2	.72	SB 251
Vermont	1920°	1924	44.2	55.8	.79	SB 252
Louisiana°°	1920°	1924	32.9	78.0	.42	SB 250 & 1920 Census

SB is Breckinridge, *Women in the Twentieth Century*.
° Illinois women had school suffrage since 1891; this was expanded to non-constitutional office (e.g., municipal elections) in 1913. Pennsylvania ratified the Nineteenth Amendment in 1919; neither Vermont or Louisiana had ratified it by August 26, 1920.
°° Louisiana data are for whites only.

of women can be tested in Oregon. County votes for suffrage in 1912 were compared with women's registration in 1917, 1919, 1921, 1922 and 1924. In these counties, no significant relationship appears between voting for suffrage in 1912 and the subsequent level of women's registration.

The possible influence of anti-suffrage sentiment, or more broadly, the persistence of the notion that women should not vote or be involved in politics, is unique to the situation surrounding the enfranchisement of women, and does not characterize the enfranchisement of other groups. Political scientists have made general claims regarding the process by which newly enfranchised people (whether enfranchised as a group, like women, or because they come of age) develop the habit of voting and a loyalty to a particular political party.[22] Tingsten's 1937 study of voting behavior

22. Among others, Herbert Tingsten, *Political Behavior: Studies in Election Statistics* (London: P. S. King & Son, 1937); Philip E. Converse, "Of Time and Partisan Stability," *Comparative Political Studies* 2 (July 1969), 139–71; Paul Allen Beck, "A Socialization Theory of Realignment"; and William Claggett, "The Life Cycle and Generational Models of the Development of Partisanship: A Test Based on the Delayed Enfranchisement of Women," *Social Science Quarterly* 60 (1980), 643–50.

after suffrage in a number of European countries found that in nearly every case, women in cities voted at a higher rate than women in rural areas, and that the difference between men's and women's voting rate was lowest in circumstances where turnout in general was the highest. Tingsten's research, which is consistent with other studies, also leads us to expect that women in certain structural or socio-economic situations would be more likely to vote than other women. Rokkan also provides examples of the kinds of factors that might affect the rates of participation of the newly enfranchised. Using Norwegian data, he demonstrates that mobilization, or integration into the political system (i.e., participation in elections and membership in parties), takes place first for new entrants who are at the "center" of society—those in more industrialized, urban, modern areas—and proceeds most slowly for those on the geographic and social peripheries.[23]

Another important source of variation in both attitudes toward women's roles and in female political behavior is ethnic background. In Sumner's study, those rural counties with large Mexican populations had the lowest levels of female involvement in politics. In all the areas she studied, the differences in voting rates between men and women who were naturalized citizens were far greater than the overall differences between men's and women's voting rates. Merriam and Gosnell found that the proportion of women who cited opposition to female suffrage as a reason for not voting was highest among women of foreign parentage, particularly of German, Irish, and Italian extraction. "The women voted in relatively larger numbers in those wards where rental values were the highest and where the proportion of foreign-born was the lowest. . . . [A]n unduly large proportion of the nonvoting adult citizens were women of foreign extraction living in the poorest residential sections of the city."[24]

Finally, traditional attitudes about women's roles seemed also to be more prevalent among the working classes, as noted by Merriam

23. Tingsten, *Political Behavior;* Stein Rokkan, "The Mobilization of the Periphery: Data on Turnout, Party Membership and Candidate Recruitment in Norway," in *Citizens, Elections, Parties,* ed. Stein Rokkan (New York: David McKay, 1970).

24. Merriam and Gosnell, *Non-Voting,* 110–11; see also Sumner, *Equal Suffrage,* 114–17.

and Gosnell. Sumner found that women turned out at a higher rate in the wealthier sections of Denver. In Chicago, Goldstein found a positive association between social class and female turnout for presidential elections, though the relationship was reversed for mayoral elections. Breckinridge cited a study of Minnesota, conducted by the League of Women Voters, which found that "the poorest voting record was held by women in domestic service."[25]

In addition to social or demographic factors, we need to consider the intentional actions of women's organizations and political parties. This is perhaps the most significant aspect of the "local conditions" to which New York's Republican women referred, but it has mostly been neglected by researchers who study newly enfranchised citizens. Political scientists have repeatedly found that organizational involvement increases political participation, and have speculated that one of the reasons for the current decline in turnout is that political parties no longer serve the important mobilizing functions that they did in previous eras.[26] And there are numerous suggestions in contemporary accounts of the 1920s that the mobilizing efforts of the parties and of women's organizations had a strong effect on the participation of women at the mass level. In Merriam and Gosnell's study, "detailed studies of certain typical precincts brought to light the fact that women's political clubs have aroused an interest in voting among a very large proportion of adult female citizens of native parentage living in the best residential districts, and that the party organizations in working-class districts were very successful in bringing out a large proportion of the male vote, and, while less successful with the women voters, were improving in this respect."[27]

Butler found higher female turnout in 1924 in those New York counties where women had traditionally been active in civic organi-

25. Sumner, *Equal Suffrage*, 110; Goldstein, *The Effects of the Adoption of Woman Suffrage*, 110–20; Breckinridge, *Women in the Twentieth Century*, 248.

26. See, for example, Sidney Verba, Norman H. Nie, and Jae-On Kim, *Participation and Political Equality: A Seven-Nation Study* (New York: Cambridge University Press, 1978); and Steven J. Rosenstone and John Mark Hansen, *Mobilization, Participation, and Democracy in America* (New York: Macmillan, 1993).

27. Merriam and Gosnell, *Non-Voting*, 255–56. Some women's groups in Chicago urged their members *not* to vote in primaries, as it would limit their political independence.

zations of all types and where these organizations were actively "encouraging their members to take part in the political life of the community."[28] At times even organizations that had been against suffrage urged women to vote. In Alabama, the Southern Women's League for the Rejection of the Anthony Amendment, for example, said in 1920 that "the time for debating the rights and wrongs of the amendment has passed and now it is time for the women to qualify as voters."[29] In San Diego, 45% of a sample of women who belonged to the PTA registered to vote, as compared to only 37% of a comparable sample of women with elementary school children who did not belong to the PTA.[30]

In summary, the literature on woman suffrage and European studies of the political integration of newly enfranchised citizens, particularly women, lead us to focus on socio-demographic factors to explain variations in levels of registration and voting, and lead us to expect that middle-class, native-born, urban women would register and vote at a higher rate than lower-class, foreign-stock, or rural women. Other political science research points us toward an examination of parties and other organizations and their efforts to mobilize women voters.

SOME CASE STUDIES

The hypotheses suggested above are difficult to test without registration and voting data which have been kept separately for men and women. In a few areas, such data exist and can be combined with census data to conduct some empirical investigations of the variations in women's political behavior during the era after suffrage. As mentioned above, Illinois had men and women use separate ballots from 1913 to 1920 (apparently it was the only state to do so: a proposal in Missouri to have women use separate ballots was found unconstitutional). Oregon did not have separate ballots but kept separate registration figures for men and women at least from 1917 to 1924, and it appears to be the only state that aggregated these statistics by county and published them. At the local

28. Butler, "Women Who Do Not Vote," 531.

29. Thomas, *The New Woman in Alabama*, 208.

30. Jean M. Smith, "The Voting Women of San Diego, 1920," *Journal of San Diego History* 26, no. 2 (1985), 147.

level, Joel Goldstein used registration and voting data from Illinois, as well as census data by wards, to study the political behavior of women in Chicago. More recently, Gerald Gamm has conducted a painstaking study of Boston's ethnic areas, in which he is able to analyze men's and women's registration separately (though his primary focus is not on gender differences) by going back to precinct-level registration lists, which kept separate tallies of men and women.[31]

The data analyzed in the recent Oregon study[32] are based on figures published in the Oregon *Blue Book* (1917–18, 1919–20, 1921–22, 1923–24, and 1925–26), and county data from the 1920 U.S. Census. The extent to which Oregon women registered to vote varied quite substantially among the counties (as did women's involvement in Illinois and New York, as noted above). In 1917, for example, female registrants in Clatsop County, in the far northwest corner of Oregon, constituted only 32.7% of the women aged twenty-one and over. In sparsely settled Harney County, on the other hand, 796 of the 913 eligible women (87.2%) registered. Men's registration varied just as much, and in general the areas of high and low registration were the same for both sexes (between 1917 and 1922, the correlation between the percentage of women registered and the percentage of men registered ranged from .78 to .92; in 1924 it was .56).

In both states, the expectation that more cosmopolitan, urban women would take advantage of suffrage more quickly than those on the periphery is *not* borne out. In Oregon, female registration (the percentage of women over twenty-one in a county who are registered) correlated negatively with the percentage of county residents living in urban places (correlations ranged around − .50 from 1917 to 1921, dropping to − .25 and − .11 in 1922 and 1924). In the most rural counties, the mean percentage of women registered from 1917 to 1924 is 67.2%; in counties with towns of over 2500, the figure is 58.6%, while for Multnomah County (Portland), it is only 49.4%. Interestingly, however, the difference between the levels of male and female registration was least in Portland

31. Goldstein, *The Effects of the Adoption of Woman Suffrage*; Gamm, *The Making of New Deal Democrats*.

32. Andersen, "Women and the Vote in the 1920s."

(about 12 percentage points as compared to about 18 percentage points in the remaining counties). Certainly in this particular political and social context, women (and men) in Oregon's rural periphery registered to vote at higher levels than those at the urban center. However, if we judge women's integration into the political system according to standards set by their male counterparts, the women of Portland demonstrate a higher level of mobilization. Tingsten's finding that the difference between men's and women's voting rate was lowest where turnout was highest is at odds with the Oregon data.

In Illinois, voting data (though not registration data) for 1916 by county and sex appeared in the *Illinois Blue Book* for 1917 to 1919; these data were merged with 1920 Census data for Illinois counties. Contrary to what Tingsten's research suggests, in Illinois population density is inversely related to turnout for both men and women (correlations are $-.34$ and $-.30$, respectively).[33] The ratio of women voting to men voting is unrelated to the population per square mile variable. It may be that the difference between European and American party systems accounts for the difference between the present findings and Tingsten's research. That is, the centralized, nationalized European mass parties may have tended to mobilize new voters in the center, while the highly decentralized structure of American parties allows for greater local variation, and high immigrant populations in the cities helped produce lower women's turnout there.

Direct data on wealth is unavailable to test the hypothesis that women's participation varied with class, with middle-class women being more involved than working-class women. In the Oregon and Illinois analyses I used "crowding" (the number of families divided by number of dwelling units in the county) as a rough approximation of the overall socio-economic situation of county residents. Women's (and men's) registration was negatively related to crowding in all years in Oregon, strongly so in 1917, 1919 and 1921 and more weakly after that. In Illinois as well, women's (and men's) turnout showed a strong negative association with crowding. Thus to the extent that data on crowding can be substituted for

33. The magnitude of the negative correlations increases when Cook County (Chicago) is eliminated from the analysis.

direct measurements of class or wealth, the hypothesis that wealthier women (and men) tend to be more integrated into the political system is supported.

Gamm's study of Boston also supports the class hypothesis. In the Jewish communities he studied, for example, in 1924 only 8.7% of the working-class Jewish women were registered, in contrast to 25.2% of the lower middle-class Jewish women and 33.2% of the upper middle-class Jewish women. Similarly, just over a third of the women in precincts Gamm labels "poor" Irish were registered, compared with over half of those in the working-class or middle-class precincts.[34]

Both Oregon and Illinois had small minority populations. Blacks comprised 2.9% of the Illinois population in 1920, and were concentrated mostly in Chicago. Oregon was also predominantly white: there were few Asians (except in Portland and Astoria), few blacks, and relatively few Indians. Just 13% of the population were foreign born (white), but almost 35% had been born abroad or had foreign-born parents. More of the residents of Illinois had been born abroad (19%) and somewhat fewer had foreign-born parents (31%). No significant relationship existed in either state between the percentage of minorities and levels of registration. The association between ethnicity and political involvement, however, is clear. In every year in Oregon, the percentage of foreign-born residents in the county population is negatively associated with the percentage of men and women over age twenty-one who were registered to vote. This association is significant in all years for men and from 1917 to 1921 for women. The fact that the association is always stronger for men may reflect the higher level of institutionalization of their voting behavior. In Illinois, the correlation between the percent of foreign-born residents and turnout is over $-.70$ for women and men.

The percentage of foreign-born county residents bears a distinct relationship, in Oregon, to the ratio variable: in all years (with $p < .05$ in 1921 and 1924) the percentage of foreign-born residents is *positively* related to the ratio of women to men registered. In Illinois, however, the percentage of foreign-born residents is nega-

34. Gamm, *The Making of New Deal Democrats*, chs. 2 and 6.

tively related to the ratio of women to men, while the percentage of native-born residents and the percentage of Black residents are positively related. Thus, in Oregon counties with high proportions of foreign-born residents (primarily those in the northwest, in the Columbia and Willamette valleys) had lower rates of voter registration, but these were the very counties where women were more highly mobilized in relation to men. Recently Courtney Brown has found that in 1920 women were mobilized at a relatively higher rate in areas with high populations of immigrant stock.[35] The reason for this, he suggests, is that male-dominated party organizations in such areas encouraged the participation of native, middle-class women in order to counter the voting strength of immigrants. The present findings, at least for Oregon, seem to be consistent with his interpretation.

The hypotheses that can be derived from the political science literature on the mobilization of new voters, for the most part, posit relationships between demographic characteristics and political behavior, as we have seen. But a focus on these demographic variables can obscure the role that parties and other organizations play in mobilizing particular groups. In Oregon and Illinois, as in other states, women were differentially attended to and mobilized by the political parties.[36]

Like men, women in these particular states registered and voted disproportionately Republican in these years. Brown's work suggests, in this context, that places where Republican organizations were already strong would see more women registering and voting, but the Oregon situation does not completely fit this model and the 1916 Illinois data are directly at odds with it. In Oregon, the association between party strength (measured by the percentage of male registrants in either the Republican or Democratic parties) and mobilization of women (the percentage of women registered) changes over the period studied. In 1917 and 1919, years when the registration data were taken from the registration books prior to

35. Courtney Brown, *Ballots of Tumult: A Portrait of Volatility in American Voting* (Ann Arbor: University of Michigan Press, 1991), ch. 6.

36. Felice Gordon's research on New Jersey, for example, shows that most of the leading suffragists in that state became active Republicans, while in Connecticut the minority Democratic party was more sympathetic to women and attracted more of them. See Gordon, *After Winning;* Nichols, *Votes and More for Women.* Brown's *Ballots of Tumult,* ch. 6, is also relevant.

special elections (e.g., referendum votes), the areas where Republicans were particularly strong tended to have lower mobilization of women. In contrast, counties where the minority Democrats were more numerous (though they were never in the majority) saw higher proportions of women registering. This is consistent with the finding above that registration of women was higher in rural Oregon counties.

The 1922 registration data, in contrast, reflect the political situation surrounding the controversial general election of 1922. The Ku Klux Klan began successfully organizing in the state in 1921, and in the spring of 1922 nearly defeated the Republican governor in the primary election. The Klan then supported the Democratic nominee, Walter Pierce, for governor in the general election; it also supported the Compulsory School Bill, a measure introduced as an initiative in the 1922 election which would have required all children between ages six and sixteen to be sent to public schools, effectively destroying private and parochial education in the state. In addition, the Klan supported Japanese exclusion and regulation prohibiting aliens from owning land. Both Pierce and the school bill won in the 1922 election, as did the Democratic (and Klan-supported) candidate from the Third District (Portland).

In this political context, it appears that the Republicans in 1922 were more successful at mobilizing women voters: in contrast to the previous data, there is a significant *positive* association between Republican strength and women's registration. That women may have been activated by the controversies around immigration, religion, and schooling, is further suggested by the fact that in 1922, in areas where Democratic strength was highest, women tended to be disproportionately Republican in their registration.[37] In addition, if we focus on the change in women's registration by creating a "change variable" (the average percent registered in 1922 and 1924 minus the average in 1917 and 1919), we find significant correlations averaging .40 between Republican strength and change in women's registration.[38] Those counties where Republicans were

37. The correlation between the percentage of males registered as Democrats and the ratio of female to male Republican strength is .31 (p <.10).

38. Regression analysis on the Oregon data reinforces the idea that demographic variables (in particular, the extent of urbanization) were important in explaining womens mobilization between 1917 and 1921, but it also makes clear that the politics of the 1922 election created a context in which women were effectively mobilized

particularly strong in relation to the opposition saw the greatest increase in women's registration.[39]

In Illinois in 1916, the Republican party was strong (as measured by percentage of Republican vote among males) in those areas where female turnout was lowest and where the ratio of women to men was also low; these tended also to be areas with high populations of foreign-born residents. In contrast, Democratic strength was associated with higher turnout of women and a higher ratio of women's to men's turnout. Obviously conclusions from these data are limited by the fact that we have only one time point.

It seems from the analysis of the Illinois and Oregon data that one of the factors that accounted for variations in women's voting rates was the extent to which one or both major parties found it advantageous to mobilize women voters.[40] This was the case elsewhere as well. In New Mexico, for example, Jensen's research shows that Hispanic women, in contrast to Anglo women, became rapidly politicized. Though voter turnout in Hispanic counties dipped from 84% in 1916 to 59% in 1920, it jumped to 68% in 1924 and rapidly grew back up to 83% by 1936. The Hispanic Republican political machine, says Jensen, quickly incorporated women, who "moved rapidly into this voting structure."[41] In New Jersey the Republican party's early recognition that most of the active suffragists tended to support Republicans, and their quick organizational responses to suffrage, explained in part why

---

by the Republicans. By 1924, the model no longer explains women's participation: while predicting the level of women's registration in earlier years produced R^2 values ranging from .33 to .44, the R^2 for 1924 was only .04.

39. The religious controversy also apparently contributed to the defeat of two Democratic women who were running for the state legislature. One of these candidates defied her party by taking a stand against the compulsory education bill, and the other thought that she would have won "if this most irreligious question had not been injected into the election" (Woman Citizen, 2 December 1922, 27); and see Robert E. Burton, Democrats of Oregon: The Pattern of Minority Politics, 1900–1956 (Eugene: University of Oregon Press, 1970) and John M. Swarthout, "Oregon: Political Experiment Station," in Western Politics, ed. Frank H. Jonas (Salt Lake City: University of Utah Press, 1961).

40. See Rosenstone and Hansen, Mobilization, Participation, and Democracy for a recent discussion of the behavior of parties and elites in mobilizing particular groups.

41. Joan M. Jensen, "'Disfranchisement is a Disgrace': Women and Politics in New Mexico, 1900–1940," New Mexico Historical Review 56 (January 1981), 25–26.

women's voting in 1920 was disproportionately Republican. In addition, as Gordon points out, the old-stock, wealthier women (who were Republicans) may have been quicker to vote than the "newer Americans," whose loyalties were more likely to the Democrats.[42] In Connecticut, in contrast, it appears that the dominance of the Republican party, and the conservatism of male GOP leaders, produced a situation where the mobilization of women was seen as politically unnecessary.[43]

Anna Harvey's recent research also supports the conclusion that political context is critical in understanding the variability in women's mobilization in the 1920s. She bases her analysis on partisan bias and mobilization elasticities, which give a sense of how a particular party's strength increases within a particular group as that group becomes more mobilized. Her data are from Boston and from various Pennsylvania cities and counties. She finds that women who were beginning to mobilize showed a bias toward the dominant party in their area and that they "contributed disproportionately to that dominant party's electoral mobilization during this period, relative to men."[44] More interesting for the present argument, she finds significant gender differences, even for men and women living in the same ethnically homogeneous neighborhoods. For example, newly mobilizing Boston Jewish women were significantly less Republican than their male counterparts, and rural Pennsylvania women were more Republican than males in the same counties. Thus she concludes that while women did not form distinct voting blocs, neither was their political behavior identical to the men living nearby: "the precise nature of women's distinctive registration behavior varied according to ethnicity and partisan context."[45]

What can we learn from this analysis of women's participation in Oregon and Illinois, and from the other research I have cited? Very simply, the data indicate that women did not vote identically

42. Gordon, *After Winning*, 81–82.

43. Nichols, *Votes and More for Women.*

44. Anna Harvey, "Uncertain Victory: The Electoral Incorporation of Women into the Republican Party, 1920–1928," paper presented at the American Political Science Association meetings, Washington, D.C., 1992, 13.

45. *Ibid.,* 11.

to men, and suggest that we cast a skeptical eye on claims that women voted according to their husbands' preferences. Neither are women a homogeneous group. Most important, the variations in the level and direction of women's mobilization in the 1920s, while certainly based in part on socio-demographic differences, are best understood as a result of political parties (and other organizations, such as women's groups) acting in specific contexts to bring women into (or keep them out of) the local voting universe.

LEARNING THE HABIT OF VOTING

Most of the studies mentioned above are in the nature of snapshots—examinations of the voting behavior of women in a particular place at a particular time. Another important question has to do with the rate at which women became integrated into the electoral system. Despite overblown predictions on the part of both suffragists and their opponents, most observers realized that the incorporation of women into the male world of politics would involve a relatively slow *learning* process. "The hope of a woman's vote, it would seem, lies in habit," said one observer in the middle of the decade.[46] This is consistent with political science research on how new citizens acquire partisan loyalties and become involved in politics. Converse, for example, predicts the aggregate level of partisanship of age cohorts by using factors such as the length of time they have been able to vote, their "inherited" partisanship, and the assumed resistance of older voters to the acquisition of new behaviors.[47] This type of analysis is problematic for women, however, and indicates why viewing women as simply one instance of the class of "newly enfranchised voters" is inadequate. Women were not merely *un*practiced at voting or *un*socialized (as were, for example, nonpropertied males in some states in the early nineteenth century). Rather, they had grown up learning that women were *by nature unsuited* to politics, that by definition politics was a male concern. In other words, there was a distinct boundary between appropriate male and female roles in the public realm, and in order to alter that boundary women had not only to learn

46. Katherine F. Gerould, "Some American Women and the Vote," *Scribner's Magazine* 77 (May 1925), 452.
47. Converse, "Of Time and Partisan Stability."

new habits, but to unlearn old assumptions about acceptable behavior.

Many politicians, journalists, and scholars writing in the twenties commented on both the necessity of habituating women to political activity, particularly voting, and on the variations in the rate at which this political learning progressed. Marguerite Wells, for example, writing in 1929, pointed out that women were gradually acquiring "voting habits" and that this was "precisely what is to be expected."[48] The League of Women Voters also heeded a learning-based argument: "an effort was particularly directed to the problem of arousing her interest and stimulating her participation before the habit of indifference should be deeply graven on her political character."[49] As one woman wrote in *Scribner's* in 1924, "Each time I vote, I am more resolved never to do it again. It is all a question, every year, of the moral influence of my husband. . . . I bow to a conviction that I do not myself feel. The sense that it is a duty to vote is simply not in me . . . I am not mentally a citizen yet. Nor, for that matter, are most of the women who have been enfranchised only since 1920."[50]

Theodora W. Youmans, who ran unsuccessfully in the Republican primary for the Wisconsin State Senate, wrote of the difficulty of learning the habit of voting. "It is idle to deny that while a little highly intelligent and public-spirited minority of women is wide-awake to the responsibility of good citizenship, and has a considerable following among less strenuous souls, the majority of women in this district are not wholly enfranchised in spirit." In one village, her workers had canvassed all the women and expected 150 votes; she received only 55. One worker said, apparently with some exasperation, "They said it was too hot. They were making jelly!" Mrs. Youmans added, "Indeed, I found jelly a third competitor of no mean significance."[51]

Tingsten's earlier research into voting patterns in Europe frames some expectations about the changes we might expect to see in

48. Marguerite M. Wells, "Some Effects of Woman Suffrage," *Annals of the American Academy of Political Science* 143 (1929), 207.

49. Breckinridge, *Women in the Twentieth Century*, 247.

50. Gerould, "Some American Women," 449.

51. *Woman Citizen*, 21 October 1922, 26.

the U.S. data during the period after suffrage. He analyzed data showing the voting participation of men and women from the time woman suffrage had been granted in particular countries to the 1930s. For example, in Finland full suffrage was granted in 1901; in Norway women received municipal suffrage in 1898 and "political" suffrage in 1907. In seven of the ten instances where he presented time series of more than four elections (these represent time periods ranging from seven to thirty-five years), the difference between the percentage of men voting and the percentage of women voting decreased over time.[52] Thus previous research would lead us to expect a gradual increase in American women's voting during the 1920s. Table 3.2 summarizes some diverse data that help describe this trend. While the geographical differences are clear, in each case there is an increase in the proportion of the electorate that is female. The rate of change for each two-year election cycle varies from 3.1% in Louisiana (where women remained a much smaller part of the electorate) to .8% in Pennsylvania. Gerald Gamm's study of registration and voting in Boston during the twenties shows the same sort of pattern, as illustrated in Table 3.3. These data illustrate the class and ethnic differences in women's voting rates as discussed above, but at the same time clearly show that Boston women in all social and ethnic groups made quite dramatic progress toward political integration during the decade of the twenties. Middle-class Jewish women and Black women, for example, were registered at a rate of about 13% in 1920, in contrast to about 30% eight years later. Gamm estimates that a quarter of the eligible "Yankee" women were registered in 1920, which increased to 62% in 1928. Women living in poor Irish precincts increased their registration from 11% to 45% in those eight years. While the absolute level of mobilization varied widely by class and ethnicity, the movement toward higher levels of participation was consistent and uniform. The changes are steady and unidirectional: they show us the beginning of a process that culminated in the 1960s and 1970s, when gender differences in turnout finally vanished.

52. Tingsten, *Political Behavior*, ch. 1. Also see Glenda Eileen Morrison, "Women's Participation in the 1928 Presidential Campaign" (Ph.D. thesis, University of Kansas, 1978), 248.

3.2 Women as Proportion of Electorates

Year	Louisiana	Rhode Island	Vermont	Pennsylvania	Hawaii	Chicago
1914						32.3%
1916						35.6
1918						36.7
1920	18.2%	38.9%	24.2%		35.1%	37.8
1922	19.9	40.2	41.1		38.0	36.5
1924	28.4	44.1	44.2	41.8%	37.9	38.5
1926	29.1	42.8	44.8	43.9	37.5	36.4
1928	30.5	45.2	47.2	46.0	38.7	43.2
1930		45.4	46.9	44.4	38.9	41.7
1932			47.2	45.2	40.8	
1934			47.2	45.2	41.2	
1936			47.6	46.4	41.5	

Sources: Breckinridge, *Women in the Twentieth Century*, pp. 249–252; Breckinridge, "The Activities of Women outside the Home," p. 739; *New York Times*, 21 October 1928 sec. 10, p. 8 and 29 October 1928, p. 2; *Vermont State Manual*; Robert C. Schmitt, *Historical Statistics of Hawaii* (Honolulu: University Press of Hawaii, 1977).

3.3 Percentage of Women Registered in Boston Ethnic Neighborhoods

Group	1920	1924	1928	1932	1936
Working-class Jews	3.2%	8.7%	15.3%	21.6%	25.8%
Lower-middle-class Jews	13.4	25.2	30.0	33.2	39.1
Upper-middle-class Jews	14.3	33.2	30.9	41.3	49.2
East Boston Italians	5.1	14.1	15.3	25.0	32.8
North End Italians	0.7	4.8	7.4	10.2	27.8
Blacks	10.8	25.5	29.5	30.6	44.5
Yankees	25.3	45.7	62.8	56.4	58.8
Poor Irish	10.6	29.1	45.2	47.5	53.6
Lower-class Irish	18.2	46.6	60.5	62.5	68.4
Working-class Irish	16.7	43.3	59.9	56.7	64.6
Lower-middle-class Irish	24.3	49.6	58.0	56.8	66.7

Source: Gerald H. Gamm, *The Making of New Deal Democrats*, tables 2.4, 3.1, 4.3, 5.4, 6.2. Registration figures for Yankees are an estimate of registration for non-servant women.

THE 1928 ELECTION: A TURNING POINT?

For a variety of reasons, the Presidential election of 1928 appears to be a turning point in the gradual process that eliminated voting as a distinguishing characteristic of the boundary between male and female political behavior. The League of Women Voters sponsored weekly radio broadcasts on politics; these were thought to have increased women's interest in the campaign, particularly those in remote areas.[53] Certainly commentators at the time perceived the election to be of particular interest to women, and the papers were once more full of predictions about the likely impact of the women's vote. There were several reasons for this perception; perhaps the most significant was the moral thrust of the campaign as it progressed, focusing on the issues of prohibition, immigration, and ethnic and religious tolerance, which were thought to be close to women's hearts. Even though the previous eight years should have made it clear that women did not vote in a monolithic bloc, this image was repeatedly resurrected during 1928, when it was routinely assumed that the great majority of women would vote for Hoover.[54]

A more careful look at women's past voting record and registration levels by region, however, suggests a more variegated picture of the probable impact of the female vote in 1928. Less visible than the clubwomen for Hoover was another phenomenon: the entry of immigrant-stock women into the active electorate on the side of the Democrats. A few writers commented on this at the time. Eunice Fuller Barnard, in the *New York Times Magazine*, questioned the assumption that all women were dry and would vote for Hoover, suggesting that this myth had developed because a few women had been vocal leaders in the temperance movement. But she reminded readers that prominent Republican women favored repeal or modification, and that some women prohibitionists (like Nellie Tayloe Ross of Wyoming) favored Smith on the basis of other issues. Other writers spoke of Smith's strengths among women factory workers, social workers, and farmers.[55] Some polls (for example, those by the *Chicago Tribune* and an extensive Hearst newspaper poll) also found support for Smith among women.[56] Immigrant women, who according to Merriam and Gos-

53. Eunice Fuller Barnard, "The Woman Voter Gains Power," *New York Times Magazine*, 12 August 1928, pp. 1–2, 20; Morrison, *Women's Participation in the 1928 Presidential Campaign*, ch. 7; and Sarah Schuyler Butler, "After Ten Years," *Woman's Journal* (April 1929), 10–11.

54. See Paul Craig Taylor, "The Entrance of Women into Party Politics: The 1920s" (Ph.D. thesis, Harvard University, 1967), 280–84.

55. Barnard, "The Woman Voter Gains Power"; McCormick, "Enter Women, the New Boss of Politics."

56. Morrison, *Women's Participation in the 1928 Presidential Campaign*, 249–63.

nell formed an important factor in women's nonvoting in 1924, were becoming naturalized citizens (and hence eligible to vote) at an increased rate during the 1920s. In the nation as a whole, only 9% of those who became naturalized citizens in 1924 were women, while 17% of those in 1926 and 25% in 1928 were women.[57] This trend created a larger pool of potential female voters, and post-election analyses indicated that "women who had never before voted had turned out in remarkable numbers. This was notably true of women whose cultural patterns had most discouraged participation in the past—Irish and New Immigrant Catholics in the North, old stock Republicans in the South."[58] Burner's research, based on unpublished Boston census reports, confirms a sharp rise in female registration in heavily Italian and Irish census tracts; he also cites newspaper accounts of heavy turnouts of women voters in New York City and in North Carolina.[59]

In many areas both parties benefited from the upsurge in women's enrollment. In Philadelphia, women constituted only 32.2% of the registered electorate in 1927, but these numbers had increased to 41.6% of the electorate just a year later. In Baltimore, the number of men registered as Republicans increased by 13% between 1924 and 1928, while the number of female Republicans rose by 62%! Similarly, male Democratic registrants were up 25%, but their female counterparts increased their numbers by 61%. In Portland, Oregon, both parties saw approximately a 10% increase in the number of men registered between 1924 and 1928, while women's Democratic registration increased by 21% and women's Republican registration increased by 27%.[60]

Post-election analyses indicated that there had indeed been a significant increase in the proportion of women voting. "Women were estimated to be 49 percent of the possible electorate in 1928 . . . up from an estimated 35 percent in 1924 and approxi-

57. Butler, "After Ten Years," 11.

58. William M. Harbaugh, "The Republican Party, 1893–1932," in *History of U.S. Political Parties,* vol. 3, ed. Arthur M. Schlesinger, Jr. (New York: Chelsea House, 1963), 2118.

59. Burner, *The Politics of Provincialism,* 229–30. Gamm, in *The Making of New Deal Democrats,* finds that this picture of an upsurge in female Democratic enrollment is true of the Irish precincts he studies, but not of the Italian areas.

60. *New York Times,* 21 October 1928, 6.

mately 30 percent in 1920."[61] According to Indiana Republican women, the women's vote in that state in 1928 was 153,000 above that in 1924, while the men's vote remained unchanged.[62]

The importance of the 1928 election in mobilizing women on both sides of the partisan fence to vote, many for the first time, emphasizes the importance of placing the behavior of any newly enfranchised group into its political context. Deciding whether to vote is a choice made not in the abstract, but in the context of particular candidate choices, party images, and issue agendas. The 1920s represented the nadir of a long process of electoral demobilization that began with the election of 1896. As Burnham argues: "This 'system of 1896,' as Schattschneider calls it, led to the destruction of party competition throughout much of the United States, and thus paved the way for the rise of the direct primary. It also gave immense impetus to the strains of antipartisan and antimajoritarian theory and practice. . . . By the decade of the 1920s this new regime and business control over public policy in this country were consolidated. During that decade hardly more than one-third of the eligible adults were still core voters."[63]

Burnham stresses here and elsewhere that the decline in voter participation in the 1920s was a product not simply of the enfranchisement of women but of this larger process, including lessened party competition and the parties' attempts to avoid controversial issues.[64] Recently Paul Kleppner has used turnout trends from years before women's suffrage to predict turnout levels in the 1920s; this allows him to measure the relative contribution of female suffrage and other factors to the low turnout rates of the 1920s. He concludes that "the lack of consistent results across states belies the sufficiency of a 'female suffrage' explanation." Instead, the explanation lies in the larger political system: politics "lacked its earlier intensity and strong voter stimulus" and thus the benefits of participation were less clear, the costs relatively greater. For new members of the electorate (such as women), the cost/benefit comparison was particularly unfavorable.[65]

61. Morrison, *Women's Participation in the 1928 Presidential Campaign*, 248.
62. Taylor, *The Entrance of Women into Party Politics*, 6.
63. Burnham, "The Changing Shape of the American Political Universe," 23.
64. *Ibid.* and Burnham, "Theory and Voting Research."
65. Kleppner, "Were Women to Blame?" 641–43. See also Kristi Andersen, *The Creation of a Democratic Majority*, ch. 3, on the growth of a "nonimmunized

As the decade progressed, and as the involvement of women in politics became less of a novelty, these costs decreased for some women; the perceived benefits of participation were possibly increased by the contentious 1928 election and were certainly increased by the issues surrounding the Depression and the 1932 campaign. In 1928 journalists commented on the proliferation of women campaign workers, the ability of the radio to bring politics to the most isolated homes, and women's altered view of politics: "their earlier inhibitions and fears are giving way, so that they are seeing politics as less of a grim duty and more of a game."[66] Other contemporary observers also perceived generational differences among women: "Women who went through the fight for equal suffrage are inclined to be skeptical and more nonpartisan than men. . . . Women who inherited the vote without effort on their part are likely to be partisans; they were enfranchised into a party rather than into citizenship per se."[67] The next chapter takes a closer look at women's involvement with the Democratic and Republican parties during the 1920s. Merriam and Gosnell noted that attitudes against women's voting (which constitute a cost of participation in Kleppner's terms,) were "still found to some extent among the older women, but they were beginning to die out in the new generation."[68]

---

population" in the 1920s: a segment of the population to which the old party alignments seemed irrelevant, who had little party loyalty, and who participated at low levels.

66. Barnard, "The Woman Voter Gains Power," 1.
67. McCormick, "Enter Women, the New Boss of Politics," 3.
68. Merriam and Gosnell, Non-Voting, 111.

"The Grand Rush of the Reception Committee"
(From *Literary Digest*, August 28, 1920, p. 11.)

FOUR   Women in Party Politics

There is no doubt that Mrs. Carrie Chapman Catt sounded the doom of feminism for many years to come when she urged the newly enfranchised American women . . . "to work for the party of your choice"—exactly where men party leaders wanted them, bound, gagged, divided, and delivered to the Republican and Democratic parties.

Anne M. Martin (suffragist, Senate candidate from Nevada), in "Feminists and Future Political Action," 1925

By looking at women's entry into party politics in the decade of the 1920s, we can begin to see how a clear and long-standing boundary was shifted, renegotiated, and re-established (though never so solidly as before). What had been an almost purely male domain was invaded by women, but disappointments awaited the new arrivals as new boundaries were quickly established.

The Democratic and Republican parties acted during the late nineteenth and early twentieth centuries essentially as obstacles to women's suffrage, in large part because important interests within both parties (e.g., liquor distributors and textile manufacturers) opposed suffrage. Both Lucy Stone's American Women's Suffrage Association (AWSA) and the National Women's Suffrage Association (NWSA), led by Elizabeth Cady Stanton and Susan B. Anthony, lived through embittering disappointments with political parties at both state and national levels. Kansas women, for example, were drawn into party politics when they were given partial suffrage in 1887, only to have the parties withdraw their support for suffrage in 1894. As Flexner describes it, "Despite the wrath of the national suffrage leadership, the Kansas women stuck to their party rather than to the measure aimed at enfranchising them, and thereby sealed its doom."[1] Neither party included a suffrage plank in their platform until 1916. Even when suffrage seemed inevitable, after 1912, "no major party ever actively or enthusiastically supported woman suffrage. Instead, parties simply ceased to obstruct it. . . . Women secured a place in our 'democracy' without the aid of political parties." Carrie Chapman Catt summed it up in 1917: "It has been the aim of both dominant parties to postpone woman suffrage as long as possible. Many of us have deep and abiding distrust of all political parties; they have tricked us so often that our doubts are natural."[2]

Moreover, partisan politics (and for virtually all Americans, politics was inextricably identified with party) was a "male sport" right up until the passage of the Nineteenth Amendment. Paula Baker says that

> Partisan politics characterized male political involve-
> ment, and its social elements help explain voters' enthu-
> siastic participation. Parties and electoral politics united
> all white men, regardless of class or other differences,
> and provided entertainment, a definition of manhood,
> and the basis for a male ritual. . . . Employing symbols
> that recalled glorious old causes . . . men advertised
> their partisanship. They took part in rallies, joined local
> organizations, placed wagers on election results, read
> partisan newspapers, and wore campaign paraphernalia.
> In large and small cities military-style marching compa-
> nies paraded in support of their party's candidates, while
> in rural areas picnics and pole raisings served to express
> and foster partisan enthusiasm.[3]

McGerr has also vividly described male political rituals, while pointing out that women were not completely excluded from parti-

1. Eleanor Flexner, *Century of Struggle: The Woman's Rights Movement in the United States* (New York: Harper & Brothers, 1974), 223.

2. Patricia L. Sykes and Julianna S. Gonen, "The Semi-Sovereign Sex: U.S. Parties as Obstacles to the Women's Movement, paper presented at the Annual Meeting of the Midwest Political Science Association (Chicago, 1991), 23; Catt quotation is from M. G. Peck, *Carrie Chapman Catt: A Biography* (New York: H. W. Wilson, 1944), 283.

3. Baker, "The Domestication of Politics," 628.

san politics. Their work, however, served mainly to support that of the men: they made food, sewed banners, and sometimes dressed up to ride on a parade float. When a woman was chosen in 1895 as a delegate from New York to the convention of the National League of Republican Clubs in Chicago, "so unprecedented was this step that it was deemed necessary for her to take a chaperon to the convention."[4]

Though both Democrats and Republicans had sometimes created small women's organizations during elections (particularly after women could vote in some states), the first visible women in the national party organizations appeared in 1892: in that year there were three women alternates to the Republican national convention, two from the new state of Wyoming.[5] In 1900 one woman sat as a delegate to the Republican convention, while "the [only] lady delegate" to the Democratic convention gave a seconding speech for William Jennings Bryan's nomination.[6] Third parties seemed more hospitable to women: at the Progressive convention in 1912, one observer wrote, there were "plenty of women delegates . . . doctors, lawyers, teachers, professors, middle-aged leaders of civic movements or rich young girls who had gone in for settlement work." The *New York Times,* in fact, ridiculed the Progressives as "managed by women and has-beens."[7]

As for party committees, Emily Newell Blair in 1929 pointed out that in some states party structures were constituted by state law, in others by precedent, and that "before suffrage was extended to women, the law, in some states, used the word 'man' or 'male,' thus limiting eligibility to these committees. Precedent always did."[8] Clearly, the idea that political parties were exclusively male entities would be difficult to alter. Carrie Chapman Catt, in an address to the 1920 convention at which NAWSA became the Na-

4. McGerr, "Political Style and Women's Power," 867; *Woman Citizen,* 29 February 1920.

5. Josephine L. Good, *Republican Womanpower: The History of Women in Republican National Conventions and Women in the Republican National Committee* (Washington, D.C.: Republican National Committee, 1963), 7.

6. Breckinridge, *Women in the Twentieth Century,* 277.

7. Miller, *Ruth Hanna McCormick,* 54–55; Gustafson, "The Women of 1912."

8. Emily Newell Blair, "Women in the Political Parties," *Annals of the American Academy of Political Science* 143 (1929), 217.

tional League of Women Voters, predicted that having the vote would not be sufficient to propel women into the male-dominated parties: "Men will say that it is right for women to vote, but when it comes to administrative work within the party, that is still the exclusive man's business." A more homespun version of this was said to be one of Cornelia Bryce Pinchot's favorite stories: two men are talking about suffrage, and one worries about what will happen if women get the vote. "No, Sam," says the other man, "the vote's all right. Just don't let them get into politics."[9]

Although some suffragists eschewed participation in parties (as discussed in Chapter 2), many more saw partisan activism and, if possible, leadership, as the most important path to political effectiveness. These women could use women's potential voting power to bargain with party leaders for the changes in rules and practice that would incorporate women into the parties. Both parties, though they had been lukewarm in their support of suffrage, saw the benefits of mobilizing the votes of women. Moreover, party leaders believed that women were best able to mobilize women, and proceeded to set up distinct structures within the party organizations for that purpose. Most of the suffragists who began working through the parties dismissed the idea of separate women's organizations and requested (or demanded, depending on their political style and clout) representation in the existing party structures.[10] An account of the gradual and incomplete entry of women party members into the inner circles of party influence in the early 1920s shows how boundaries were negotiated between women expecting and demanding change and men protecting the status quo.

THE PARTIES' RESPONSE TO SUFFRAGE

The national party organizations, sensitive to the demands and the potential influence of a new element in the electorate, responded to the imminent granting of suffrage with organizational changes designed to give women nominally equal roles in the party hierar-

9. *Woman Citizen*, 6 March 1920, 947; John W. Furlow, "Cornelia Bryce Pinchot: Feminism in the Post-Suffrage Era," *Pennsylvania History* 43 (October 1976), 337–38.

10. *Woman Citizen*, 6 March 1920, 941–42; *Woman Citizen*, 31 December 1921, 19.

chy and to allow for efficient mobilization of women voters by women leaders. In 1918 Republican Chairman Will H. Hays asked Ruth Hanna McCormick of Illinois to head a National Women's Executive Committee of the Republican National Committee. A Women's Division was created in the same year, headed first by McCormick, then by Christine Bradley South of Kentucky.

At the December 10, 1919 meeting of the Republican National Committee, four women, including suffragists Mary Garrett Hay from New York and Harriet Taylor Upton from Ohio, were appointed members of the Republican Council, which consisted of twenty-four members, twelve from the RNC and twelve from outside the Committee. This meeting also proposed a Rules Change to be considered by the 1920 national convention: that the size of the RNC be doubled, and that each state should be entitled to one man and one woman member. It was further suggested that this principle of representation "be advocated as the Republican Party policy in the formation of state and county committees."[11] The next month, a meeting of Republican women from fourteen midwestern states also asked that the RNC membership be doubled and that the "fifty-fifty rule" become the norm for all party committees; a similar plea was made by New York Republican women, and Mary Garrett Hay urged full recognition of women in party councils as she departed for the Republican convention in June.

At the convention, Republican women met and appointed a committee to meet with the Rules Committee and ask for equal representation on the National Committee. Eventually, however, the women agreed that endorsing "adequate" rather than "equal" representation would be less contentious. The Rules Committee "said an emphatic No," and proposed instead to expand the Executive Committee of the RNC from ten to fifteen members, to allow appointments of non-committeemen, and to urge the party chairman to appoint seven women along with eight men. They did not agree to appoint women to the Republican National Committee. "Mrs. Hay," noted a writer for the *Woman Citizen*, "isn't given to surrender, and she fought to the last ditch. But the men wouldn't budge." Republican women leaders, not wanting the Democrats

11. Good, *Republican Womanpower*, 10–11.

to benefit from their seeming unhappiness with the party, and needing to demonstrate to male party leaders that they could control their followers, accepted the compromise with reasonably good grace. "When I say I am dissatisfied, I do not mean there is dissension. There is no bitterness, no threat to bolt the party, or anything of that sort. We feel that we should have received more than has come to us so far," said Mrs. Hay, noting that there was now no immediate prospect of having national committeewomen.[12]

The 1920 Republican convention, held two months before the suffrage amendment was ratified, included 27 women delegates (2.7% of the total) and 129 alternates. Ironically, given the convention's rejection of the women's demands for equal representation on the national committee, the party platform "welcome[d] women into full participation into the affairs of government and the activities of the Republican Party." Table 4.1 illustrates trends in the number of women convention participants for both Democrats and Republicans. The percentages in this table are based on the actual number of delegates and alternates attending, without regard to the parties' tendency to "split" state votes. With split votes, used particularly by the Democrats, a state that had been allocated eight alternates might choose sixteen, with each to have one-half vote. This kind of vote-splitting was done frequently in the twenties with the intention of incorporating more women; looking at the number of delegates therefore means that women's *voting* strength in the conventions was somewhat less than the percentages would indicate. But the emphasis here is not on convention votes but rather on the numbers of women participating in the party deliberations as delegates, alternates and committee members. Republican women's attendance at the national convention increased dramatically in both 1920 and 1924. This was undoubtedly due to the GOP's desire to placate and mobilize the women's vote, as well as to the desire of many women, in the wake of suffrage, to have an active role in party politics. In 1924 women constituted 11% of the delegates and 25% of the alternates. This proportion of alternates was essentially maintained for

12. *Woman Citizen,* 28 June 1924, 2; *New York Times,* 6 January 1920, 1; *New York Times,* 11 January 1920, 16; *New York Times,* 2 June 1920, 3; *New York Times,* 7 June 1920, 6; *New York Times,* 9 June 1920, 2; *New York Times,* 10 June 1920, 6.

4.1 Women's Participation in Party Conventions, 1916–1956

	Republicans			Democrats		
Year	Delegates	Alternates	Committees[°]	Delegates	Alternates	Committees[°]
1916	5 (<1%)	9 (1%)	0	6 (<1%)	11 (1%)	0
1920	27 (3%)	129 (13%)	0	93 (7%)	206 (24%)	0
1924	120 (11%)	277 (25%)	25	199 (14%)	310 (29%)	20
1928	70 (6%)	264 (24%)	8	152 (10%)	263 (22%)	12
1932	87 (8%)	307 (27%)	17	208 (12%)	270 (19%)	8
1936	61 (6%)	222 (22%)	12	252 (15%)	333 (29%)	17
1940	78 (8%)	231 (23%)	11	208 (11%)	347 (24%)	9
1944	99 (9%)	264 (25%)	43	174 (11%)	332 (22%)	58
1948	112 (10%)	254 (23%)	55	192 (12%)	320 (24%)	59
1952	129 (11%)	260 (22%)	50	203 (12%)	322 (20%)	57
1956	208 (16%)	355 (27%)	58	287 (12%)	391 (21%)	63

[°]Major committees included are the Permanent Organization, Credentials, Rules, and Platform.

Sources: Sophonisba P. Breckinridge, "The Activities of Women Outside the Home," in *Recent Social Trends in the United States*, 741); Marguerite J. Fisher and Betty Whitehead, "Women and National Party Organization," *American Political Science Review* 38 (1944), 896; Paul T. David, Ralph M. Goldman, and Richard C. Bain, *The Politics of National Party Conventions* (Washington, D.C.: Brookings Institution, 1960); Judith H. Parris, *The Convention Problem* (Washington, D.C.: Brookings Institution, 1972); *Proceedings* of the Democratic and Republican National Conventions, various years.

Beginning in 1944, the Republican Platform Committee had one man and one woman (if possible) from each state; beginning in 1964 all the committees were so constituted, so that essentially half the committee members were women from 1964 on.

the next thirty years, while the percentage of women delegates dropped off to only six to eight percent during the period from 1928 to 1940, then crept up to 16% by 1956.

As promised, in 1920 eight women were appointed to the twenty-one member Executive Committee of the Republican National Committee: South; Upton (who was also, under the compromise worked out at the convention, vice chairman of the RNC); Katherine Phillips Edson (California); Mrs. Manley Fosseen (Minnesota): Mrs. Jeannette A. Hyde (Utah); Mrs. Arthur Livermore (New York); Ruth McCormick; and Mrs. Corinne Roosevelt Robinson (New York). At a meeting of the RNC on June 8, 1921, the post of second vice chairman of the RNC was created, and Mrs. Leonard G. Wood from Pennsylvania was elected to fill it.[13] In mid-1923

13. Good, *Republican Womanpower*, 14; *Woman Citizen*, 7 February 1920.

the RNC agreed that the (male) members would each appoint a woman "associate member" from their state. Finally, the 1924 national convention in Cleveland agreed to the enlargement of the RNC and the election of male and female members from each state. The women's struggle for this representation had been "determined and frequently embittered," and in fact the women associate members of the RNC reportedly planned a "secret conference" at the convention "at which they would draw up a protest setting forth the things which had been promised to them by the men party leaders and had not been granted, and expressing their resentment." When William Butler, incoming party chairman, and the Coolidge forces expressed their support for equal representation on the National Committee, this meeting was called off, and the next day the "Old Guard" among the Rules Committee was defeated, and the Republican women "won the prize of equal representation with men in their party councils, which was granted to their Democratic sisters in 1920."[14]

The Republican National Committee enlisted the outgoing president of the National Association of Colored Women (NACW), Hallie Q. Brown, to direct mobilization efforts among black women during the 1924 campaign. She "built her campaign network on the foundation of the existing regional, state, and local structures of her organization." One of the NACW leaders she recruited, Maria C. Lawton from Brooklyn, was also the editor and manager of the NACW's *National Notes*, and she transformed this nationally read magazine into "a political organ for the Republican party." The widespread and officially recognized network of black women's Republican clubs gave their members a strong sense of personal enrichment and political efficacy, as did Coolidge's victory in 1924. After the 1924 election Republican activists formed the National League of Republican Colored Women (NLRCW); the leader of this organization, Nannie Burroughs, was invited to the GOP's first national conference of women leaders in 1927.[15]

Meanwhile, the Democratic National Committee had created a Women's Bureau as early as 1916 to mobilize women voters in the western states where they had the franchise. The DNC agreed in

14. *Woman Citizen*, 134 July 1923, 4; *New York Times*, 8 June 1924, 3.
15. Higginbotham, "In Politics to Stay," 206–7.

February 1919 to appoint a woman associate member of the DNC from each state based on the nomination of the state committeeman. The Committee also recommended that the Democratic State Committees provide women with similar representation at the state and local level. The May meeting of the DNC was the first to include women, and the *Woman Citizen* reported that the men were relieved that their female colleagues were well-dressed, not "frumpy," and asserted that the meeting was an "education" for both sexes. The party Executive Committee met in September, reaffirming its support of the Nineteenth Amendment and adopting a resolution proposed by Mrs. George Bass, chairman of the Women's Bureau of the party, that provided for equal representation of men and women (seventeen of each) on the Executive Committee.[16]

Eleven women were appointed members of the Executive Committee of the DNC in February of 1920; six more were appointed later to make the number of women equal to that of men.[17] At the 1920 convention in San Francisco, the delegates accepted (apparently without debate) the following Rules Committee decision: the DNC would be doubled in size, and "one man and one woman hereafter should be selected from each state, the men to be chosen according to the laws of the respective States or territories, and the women to be elected this year by the delegates to the present convention and thereafter in the same manner as the men."[18]

A *New York Times* analyst wrote after the conventions of the more generous spirit with which the Democrats had accepted women and responded to their demands. "The Republican machine formed a receiving line near the front door of its party, and extended a gray-gloved hand to its women. The Democratic machine flung open all its doors, front, side, back and cellar, and wrote 'Welcome!' on each doormat." The Republicans, she suggested, were so sure of victory that they did not need to cultivate women's support at any more than a symbolic level. The minority Democrats, on the other hand, "want the woman vote, they want woman cooperation. . . . They took women into their councils, they listened not patiently and tolerantly, but eagerly to what women

16. *Woman Citizen,* 21 June 1919, 60; *Woman Citizen,* 15 November 1919.
17. *New York Times,* 16 February 1920, 15.
18. *New York Times,* 26 June 1920, 1.

said."[19] Perhaps the response of the Democrats should be considered in light of the Democratic party's somewhat greater hospitality to immigrants. The historian John Buenker says:

> The adjustment of most urban new stock legislators to the realities of woman suffrage epitomized their attitude toward political reform in general during the Progressive era. So long as the enfranchisement of women appeared to be a device favored by old stock Americans to blunt the impact of the lower-class vote and stymie attempts to alter the socioeconomic status quo, the urban machine and its constituents resisted it ferociously. Once it became apparent that the idea was politically popular, that its impact upon the machine's methods of operation would not be catastrophic, and, above all, that its enactment might actually add significantly to the growing power of the urban vote, most city politicians ceased their opposition and became open, if not avid, advocates of female voting.[20]

The Democratic women in 1920 were proud that their party had apparently been willing to concede them more equal representation than the Republican party, and the party used this to advantage, advertising in the *Woman Citizen* just before the 1920 election that the Democrats had given women organizational equality (equal numbers of men and women on the DNC) "while the Republican Organization accorded women no such recognition." The Republicans countered with an advertisement including pictures of the eight female members of the Republican National Executive Committee, described (in implicit contrast to the National Committee) as the "REAL COMMITTEE that does the work and controls the management of the biggest transaction in American politics—the Presidential election."[21]

19. Anna Steese Richardson, "Women at Two Conventions," *New York Times*, 7 July 1920, sec. 8, p. 2.

20. John D. Buenker, *Urban Liberalism and Progressive Reform* (New York: Scribners, 1973), 161.

21. *Woman Citizen*, 11 September 1920, 399; *Woman Citizen*, 9 October 1920, 513.

But despite their relatively warmer welcome by the national Democrats, the level of party commitment to women and their concerns was heavily dependent on the political skill and motivation of particular women politicians. Though a Women's Bureau had been funded and supported during the 1920 campaign, it languished afterwards until revived by Emily Newell Blair, vice president of the DNC, in 1922. She reported to the DNC that she had found "a single folder containing applications for the position of Head of the Women's Bureau and some thousands of names of unknown and untried women." Between April and September of 1922 Blair organized over 700 Democratic Women's Clubs, offered assistance to Senate and House candidates, and sent out speakers. Eventually she developed a mailing list consisting of 200 Democratic women from each county in each state.[22]

At the 1924 Democratic convention in Madison Square Garden, women had 184 votes out of 1098, or 17% of the total. Some women served as delegation chairmen. Mrs. Leroy Springs of South Carolina chaired the Committee on Credentials and was the first woman to be nominated for the vice presidency. In addition, a woman was selected (at the request of the women delegates) as one of the vice chairmen of the convention. "Although this was not the first convention which women attended," says one historian, "there were a sufficient number here to affect its color and tone. . . . [T]his was the first convention in which women served equally with men on the national committee . . ."[23] The women claimed that there were no issues on which they would take a unified and distinct stand, even prohibition, though one woman went on to say that "women will represent the largest single body in the convention that is actively sympathetic to what may be called the 'Wilson tradition.'" In several interviews women stressed their "consolidation" into the party machinery.[24]

The numbers of women participating in the national conventions in 1920 (and, to a lesser extent, in 1924) appear to confirm some differences between the parties (see Table 4.1). A total of nearly 300 women went to the Democratic convention in San Francisco,

22. *Proceedings of the Democratic Convention 1924*, 1093–96.
23. Robert Murray, *The 103rd Ballot: Democrats and the Disaster in Madison Square Garden* (New York: Harper & Row, 1976), 99–100.
24. *New York Times*, 23 June 1924, 4.

where they comprised 7% of the delegates and 24% of the alternates. This compares with the GOP's group of only 156 women, 3% of the delegates and 13% of the alternates. But by 1928 "women's place" at the conventions of both parties had been given some numerical consistency. While the Democrats tended to include more women delegates, the difference was not dramatic. More important was the fact that after the initial flurry of demands, meetings, negotiations and media attention in 1920 and 1924, the men and women of the parties more or less reached a settlement that allowed women to make up about 10% to 15% of the delegates and about a fourth of the alternates.

As mentioned in chapter 3, some observers saw 1928 as a turning point: a time when women were taken seriously rather than patronized, when they were no longer such novelties as candidates and campaign workers, and when moral issues (presumed to be women's issues) were taken up during the campaign. Others, like Emily Newell Blair, saw in the end of the decade a weakening of whatever influence women had gained with suffrage.

Certainly Republicans in particular intentionally conducted a "special women's crusade" in 1928, appealing to women "as women" and homemakers. They made strong appeals based on Hoover's experience with the Food Administration during the war. Democratic women, meanwhile, pointed to Governor Smith's endorsement of protective legislation for women and children and his appointment of women to positions in state government. Sallie Hert, vice chairman of the Republican National Committee, focused on 1928 as a watershed. "In my opinion this is the first real awakening women have had in politics. Four years ago they were barely voting." Though the numbers of women attending the national conventions had decreased somewhat from 1924, their influence had increased. Mabel Walker Willebrandt, Assistant U.S. Attorney General, chaired the Credentials Committee at the Republican convention, and of course Belle Moskowitz, as Al Smith's chief advisor, played an important role at the Democratic convention. Women at the 1928 conventions were said to be more accustomed to politics and taken more seriously by the men.[25] On the other hand

25. Eunice Fuller Barnard, "Women Who Wield Political Power," *New York Times Magazine,* 2 September 1928; Taylor, *The Entrance of Women into Party Politics,* 278–84.

Moskowitz herself said in 1930 that "the major political parties are still man-made and man-controlled. Few of their leaders can work with women on a basis of equality." And Eleanor Roosevelt said in 1928 that "beneath the veneer of courtesy and outward show of consideration universally accorded women there is a widespread male hostility—age-old, perhaps—against sharing with them any actual control."[26]

The 1928 election was indeed a turning point for black women. Daisy Lampkin of Pennsylvania, chairman of the NLRCW Executive Committee, directed the mobilization of black women voters in the East. Nannie Burroughs was appointed to the party's Speakers' Bureau and became a sought-after campaign speaker. "Many NLRCW members journeyed to Washington for the inauguration of Hoover. They rejoiced in his victory. It seemed just as much their own." This feeling of inclusion did not last, however; even at Hoover's inauguration, black campaign workers were "disinvited" from the Inaugural Ball and made to attend a segregated ball.[27] Changing leadership of the Women's Division in 1932, as well as the unresponsiveness of the Hoover administration to the economic plight of black Americans, began to loosen the ties between the black women's organizations and the GOP, though these ties were not irretrievably broken until 1936.

The national party organizations asked the state parties to afford equal representation to women, but the states varied greatly in their compliance with this request. Even within states, the two parties often differed in the extent to which women were incorporated into the party organization. In part this depended on the perceived benefit of women's votes to the state party and in part it depended on the extent to which politically active suffragists were involved with a particular party. Which party suffragists decided to support depended on the political context: in New Jersey most (though not all) of the suffragists went into the Republican party, while Nichols's study of Connecticut suffragists in the 1920s found a much larger variation. Of the twenty-nine women studied, seven were engaged in non-electoral politics only, nine were in League of Women Voters or other nonpartisan political groups, seven were active in the Democratic party, four in other parties, and only two (one

26. Belle L. Moskowitz, "Junior Politics and Politicians," *Saturday Evening Post,* 6 September 1930, 6; *New York Times,* 10 March 1928, 3.

27. Higginbotham, "In Politics to Stay," 211–12.

of whom was black, the other white) were involved in Republican politics.[28] In part this was because though the Republicans in Connecticut (like the Democrats) hoped to gain the support of women voters, they acted to prevent reform-minded former suffragists from obtaining key party positions. The male Republican leaders even appointed former anti-suffragists to the state Central Committee.[29] In New Mexico, women's Republican clubs had been organized in 1916, with the help of Dr. Jessie Russell, a prominent California suffragist, by leaders worried about the potential power of the women's vote. After the suffrage amendment was ratified, the GOP acted quickly to use these lists and recruit suffrage leaders. Three women were appointed to the eleven-member state Executive Committee, and fifty-seven women became state committeewomen, including eight former suffragists. Though the Democrats also enlarged their state committee and placed four women on the party Executive Committee, they lagged behind the Republicans (the majority party) in organizing women.[30]

By 1929, when Emily Newell Blair wrote an article on "Women in the Political Parties," eighteen states had "some sort of fifty-fifty organization in both major political parties." In the mid-1940s, Marguerite Fisher's research showed that eleven states had provided for equal representation at all levels of party committees, while eighteen more implemented the fifty-fifty rule at some levels (e.g., in the state committee but not in the county committees).[31] The Democratic party, at this point, had clearly made more progress toward sexual equality than the Republicans: of the ten states where the parties varied, in only one (Louisiana) did the GOP provide for more extensive equal representation than did the Democrats. In five states in the 1940s (New Mexico, North and South Carolina, Oklahoma, and Pennsylvania) the Democratic party had fifty-fifty arrangements for all its committees and the Republicans had no such provisions at all. Southern and some western states in particular lagged behind other states in implementing these policies; in Fisher's study Arizona,

28. Nichols, *Votes and More for Women;* Gordon, *After Winning.*
29. Nichols, *Votes and More for Women,* 40.
30. Jensen, "Disfranchisement is a Disgrace."
31. This analysis is further complicated because in some states parties are more closely regulated by state laws than in other states; hence some of the equal representation provisions were mandated by state laws, some by internal party regulations, and some by mixtures of both. This is still the case.

Georgia, Maryland, Mississippi, Nevada, North Dakota, Virginia, and Wisconsin had no equal representation policies.[32]

In the early part of the twenties there is abundant evidence that the party organizations were eager to secure the votes of women, and that organizational concessions to women were perceived as a way to do this. As early as the summer of 1919, the *Woman Citizen* had reported on a conference of national and state Democratic leaders in Iowa, "when women for the first time were admitted to the party council on the same terms as men. Two hundred of the five hundred party members present were women." In New York at about the same time, a conference of men and women party leaders in Suffolk and Nassau counties agreed to a plan to elect or appoint women to positions of authority on county and district committees within the party. New York women Republicans endorsed a fifty-fifty plan for all party committees.[33]

New Jersey parties responded quickly to suffrage. Even before ratification and the subsequent passage of legislation in 1921 that granted women the right to hold office and to serve equally on party committees, the state Republican and Democratic parties made efforts to include women in the party structures. State Republicans in May 1920 named Lillian Feickert vice chairman of the State Committee and created a Women's Division of the State Committee. By mid-1920 the Democrats had established a six-person Women's Executive Committee as an adjunct to the State Committee, but unlike the Republicans the party undertook no statewide efforts to organize women.[34]

Even though both the Illinois and Wisconsin attorneys general ruled that women could not vote for delegates to the national party conventions, state leaders of both parties assured women that they fully intended to include women in the state delegations.[35] Sometimes this was accomplished by appointing women as delegates,

32. Blair, "Women in the Political Parties," 219, 223; Lemons, *The Woman Citizen*, 87; *Woman Citizen*, 16 August 1919, 256; and Marguerite J. Fisher, "Women in the Political Parties," *Annals of the American Academy of Political and Social Science* 251 (May 1947), 89–90.

33. *Woman Citizen*, 9 August 1919, 235; also see *Woman Citizen*, 20 September 1919, 404, 410; and *Woman Citizen*, 24 January 1920, 27.

34. Gordon, *After Winning*, 78–80.

35. *Woman Citizen*, 3 January 1924; *Woman Citizen*, 7 February 1920, 808.

and Democrats in several states increased their number of at-large delegates to the convention from four to eight, giving each one-half vote, in order to have more women participate in the convention.

In New York, the state Republican convention in Rochester in 1924 included about 450 women as delegates or alternates—almost a quarter of the total. The *New York Times* reported that "Not only will their representation be larger but women appear to be coming into their own as participants in preconvention conferences of the leaders. There is hardly anything of a political character going on behind the scenes at the present convention in which women leaders are not heard."[36]

In the Tammany machine in New York, though apparently not in other urban machines, there were a number of locally powerful women politicians. In some cases they had gotten involved in politics through their fathers or husbands, but had then developed their own following. Mrs. Barbara Porges, for example, was described in 1924 as having been the boss of the Second District for nearly fifty years. Her assistance to her largely immigrant-stock constituents was famous, but her "activities are not confined merely to philanthropical deeds. Her voters are tabulated and she can tell to a man how many votes she can count upon. . . . If she says she is going to deliver the vote, it is as good as done."[37]

Clearly, things had changed since the early years of the century, when a woman had been elected as a delegate to the state Republican convention of Massachusetts and one male official, explaining why he was against seating her despite the preferences of the voters, said "suppose they had elected a trained monkey; should we be obliged to accept him?"[38]

CHANGE AND RESISTANCE: NEGOTIATING NEW BOUNDARIES

At the same time, as we have already seen in the case of the national Republican party, male party leaders clearly resisted the inclusion of women in party councils; certainly they avoided ceding real power over elections, money, or appointments to women when

36. *New York Times*, 24 September 1924, 2.
37. *New York Times*, 1 June 1924, sec. 8, p. 9.
38. *Woman Citizen*, 6 March 1920: 945.

they could. At the Democratic National Committee meeting of February 1919, in which Mrs. Bass proposed committee member- ship for women and the fifty-fifty principle at all levels, the argu- ments over the implementation of these ideas show how reluctant many men were to incorporate women wholeheartedly into the party hierarchy. Mrs. Bass proposed the selection of women associ- ate members of the DNC from each state where women could vote; these new members would be appointed by the chairman of the DNC on nomination by the respective state committeemen. After she presented her report, the Minnesota committeeman pointed out that nothing had been said about whether these women would have voting rights on the DNC, and added that he was personally in favor of women having the vote. The chairman, Homer Cummings, was clearly shocked. "I think it would be un- lawful under our practice. It never occurred to me that any one would imagine that they had a vote by reason of having been made associate members." Another committeeman pointed out that only the national convention could officially enlarge the DNC and thus give new members voting rights. The Iowa committeeman sug- gested that the DNC could dissolve itself into a conference, con- duct business with men and women voting, then resolve itself back into a committee and endorse the conference's work. "They are here to stay," he argued, "and we might as well recognize them." But Cummings persisted: "Does anyone seriously think that by creating this associate committee that there would be any rightful claim on the part of the women so appointed, that they be given a vote in our meeting?" Mrs. Bass restrained herself, and the voting issue was glossed over at this meeting; the 1920 convention, by doubling the size of the DNC, eliminated the category of associate member. By the time of the convention, incidentally, Mr. Cum- mings urged the delegates to "support this resolution without de- bate" if they were "earnest about this business of allowing the women of this country to participate fully and freely. . . ." This account illustrates perfectly how each step of women's entry into electoral and party politics was met by significant resistance and often entailed difficult negotiation of new boundaries.[39]

39. *Proceedings of the Democratic National Convention* (including the Demo- cratic National Committee) 1920: 88–89, 93, 496–501.

In Connecticut, there was conflict over admission of women to town party caucuses, in which candidates for local offices and for party conventions were selected. One woman reported that "the machine had given no opportunity to the women to vote" at Republican caucuses; the party leaders "were afraid that the men would let the women vote and so upset the cut and dried program."[40]

Atlanta in the summer of 1919 was the scene of a kind of morality play for soon-to-be-enfranchised women everywhere, a fascinating tale of political innocence, betrayal and revenge. The Democratic City Executive Committee, in anticipation of suffrage, gave Democratic women the right to vote in party primaries in May 1919, if they paid a registration fee of one dollar. A Central Committee of Women Citizens (CCWC) was formed to encourage registration and decide how to spend the registration fees. A mass meeting of women was called to vote on how to spend the money. But with the money in hand, the male leaders began backing down from their previous pronouncements. They asked for a joint committee of seven women from the CCWC and seven men from the Executive Committee to *recommend* the expenditure to the Executive Committee, which, the women were sternly reminded, retained all power to disburse the money. Conferring with the Executive Committee brought no success, and the mass meeting refused to vote on the expenditure, saying they would give up their right to vote in the primary if the Executive Committee did not honor its agreement to let the women spend the money. The Tax Collector, who was sympathetic to the women, agreed to hold the money, and in response the Executive Committee delivered an ultimatum: turn over the money or lose the vote. A meeting of women decided overwhelmingly to "stand firm." The Democratic leaders, in the end, did not dare to carry out their ultimatum, and at the primary election of September 3rd, all the members of the Executive Committee were defeated.[41]

An observer at the Republican convention in 1920 wrote that it was "interesting, too, to watch the men as they seek to compromise with the [women's] ambition, calm it, keep a lid on it. Women have so far been given no sort of adequate recognition by either of the

40. Nichols, *Votes and More for Women*, 38.
41. *Woman Citizen*, 13 September 1919, 365, 371.

major parties."[42] Yet women party loyalists were mindful of Carrie Catt's admonition that "success can only be found on the inside." In her speech to the newly formed League of Women Voters in Chicago in February of 1920, Catt was prophetic. "When you enter the parties, you will find yourself in a political penumbra where most of the men are. They will be glad to see you and you will be flattered by their warm welcome and you will think how nice it is, going to dinners and hearing grand speeches at the big political meetings . . . but if you stay long enough and move around, and keep your eyes wide open, you will discover a little denser thing, which is the numbra of the political party, the people who are planning the platforms and picking out the candidates, and doing the real work which you and the men voters sanction at the polls. You won't be so welcome there, but that is the place to be."[43]

As Catt predicted, women entered those inner chambers of the political parties only rarely, and usually only when they had some political resources of their own with which to bargain. In New Jersey, Lillian Feickert was in the advantageous position of being perceived as an influential leader of suffragist women, and thus could use her control of the potential woman vote as a bargaining chip. In 1920, the New Jersey Republican organization wanted to name Mrs. Feickert vice chairman of the State Committee. She "did not play a woman's game," however, according to the *New York Times*, but was "prepared to meet her new confreres on their own ground." In return for accepting the position and lending her political influence to the party, she apparently exacted an agreement from the party leaders that all party committees should be composed equally of men and women; that there should be women on all juries; and that at least two members of the State Board of Education and the Department of Health should be women. Her terms were accepted. New Jersey Republicans proposed a state law providing women equal representation in state and county party organizations; this bill passed in the 1921 session. The appointments to the state boards were also duly made.[44]

42. *Woman Citizen*, 12 June 1920, 41.

43. *Woman Citizen*, 6 March 1920, 947.

44. *New York Times*, 15 April 1928, sec. 10, p. 6; *New York Times*, 7 May 1923, sec. 8, p. 1; Gordon, *After Winning*, 206–7; *Woman Citizen*, 31 December 1921, 10, 19.

Ruth Hanna McCormick had learned from her father, her husband, and the many other politicians with whom she had worked over the years how to bargain with the political resources created by favors, hard work, and persuasive skills. Thus, for example, in 1928 when she was elected to Congress, she wanted a particular candidate to succeed her as Republican national committeewoman and she struck a deal with Illinois Senator Deneen. He preferred another woman, but she secured his support for her preferred candidate in return for her endorsement of his candidate for the position of national committeeman.[45]

In Connecticut, the Democratic national committeewoman in 1924, Caroline Ruutz-Rees, asked that four of the eight convention delegates-at-large be women, as the fifty-fifty rule would suggest. However, "five men had already been chosen before she was consulted about her notion of what constituted half and half." She persisted "pleasantly," and eventually Connecticut sent ten delegates-at-large to New York, five men and five women.[46]

Adelina Otero-Warren, who had developed strong political skills and a following in New Mexico during the suffrage movement, had resigned from her position as head of the state Congressional Union to become chairman of the women's division of the Republican State Committee. In 1920 she "spent three hours in the Republican caucus, reputedly the first woman to ever attend a state political caucus," and persuaded the GOP leaders to allow women to vote in the primaries and to be seated at the next convention, as well as to support ratification of the Nineteenth Amendment.[47]

On the other hand, women without the political resources of Feickert, McCormick, or Otero-Warren, or the determination of Mrs. Ruutz-Rees, frequently failed to change the party structures or have their demands met. For example, Mrs. May Lilly, a Democratic assemblywoman from the Seventh District in Manhattan and a lawyer, had introduced in 1919 a bill which gave political parties the right, if they desired, to elect one woman and one man from each assembly district in the State Committee. The bill was killed in committee on the grounds that this would make the state com-

45. Miller, *Ruth Hanna McCormick*, 194–95.
46. *New York Times*, 29 June 1924, sec. 8, p. 3.
47. Jensen, "Disfranchisement is a Disgrace," 17, 23.

mittees "too large."[48] In general, as one analyst said perceptively in 1924, the parties took women seriously who showed that they could mobilize votes for the party; a woman would rise to a leadership position who "proves that she has personal following acquired by her ability to organize, by her popularity with her group, or by her power to stir people's imaginations so that they trail after where she leads."[49]

The boundary that delineated appropriate male and female behavior was no longer drawn so that political parties were exclusively male domains, but new gendered boundaries were established within the party system. One emerging distinction, as we have seen, was between those people having real power and influence within the parties and those without such power and influence. Democratic and Republican campaign organizations recognized this in the advertisements they placed in the *Woman Citizen,* with each claiming, in effect, that women in *their* party had greater access to real decision-making power. It would have been naive to expect that hundreds of politically inexperienced women would quickly be able to achieve real influence within the parties. Rather, as with men, the extent to which women were able to penetrate into the "umbra" depended on their political resources, skills, and constituencies. The *New York Times* listed all the women delegates and alternates at the 1920 Democratic convention; of the thirty whom they profiled briefly, eleven were described as influential party activists, usually having held party office. Along with these were six former suffragists, five who were active clubwomen, three whose occupations were mentioned, and five others merely described as "leaders" or "active." For the most part, those who had political visibility and influence at this early stage had already been active in the parties, in voluntary organizations, or in suffrage organizations.[50]

Women's place within the party organizations was distinguished from men's in several other ways. At the national conventions, even though a few women may have held important committee positions

48. *Woman Citizen,* 7 June 1919, 9.

49. Anne O'Hagan Shinn, "Politics Still Masculine, Convention Women Discover," *New York Times Magazine,* 29 June 1924, 3, 11.

50. *New York Times,* 26 June 1920, 1.

or seconded nominations, as a group women were treated as special. In 1924 at the Democratic convention in Madison Square Garden, a committee was set up, under the direction of New York national committeewoman Elisabeth Marbury, to deal with both women delegates and the wives of male delegates. "This group organized special church services, special art and museum exhibits, and special tours for women."[51] In 1928, a quarter ton of candy in large packing cases labeled "Sweeten the Day with Candy" was shipped to the women delegates to the Republican National Convention at Kansas City and the Democratic convention in Houston, a gift from the National Confectioners' Association.[52] Many women active in politics seemed ambivalent about this special treatment; some were straightforwardly critical. A woman journalist in Oklahoma decried the policy of some campaign managers who "deal[t] with women on an entirely different basis. . . . They are preparing to establish at headquarters a hostess who will wear her best clothes and smile, serve tea to the callers, and entertain them with light talk. This is not equal rights, it is but holding to the old order of things that women are not capable of taking an intelligent part in things political."[53]

Even among the party elites, women saw that they were excluded from power. The Democratic National Committee consisted of one man and one woman from each state. Yet during the summer before the 1928 election, an informal meeting of male committee members chose the DNC's vice chairmen, who were women, without consulting any of the committeewomen.[54] Similarly, the Republican national committeewomen from eastern states were not invited to an important session on campaign strategy, which was held in New York and attended by all their male counterparts; "at the same time, over the protest of some of [the women], they were called to a women's meeting in Washington."[55]

At the local level, although women served in many areas as state and county committeewomen, they were often assigned responsi-

51. Murray, *The 103rd Ballot,* 99.
52. *New York Times,* 8 June 1928, 2.
53. *Woman Citizen,* 23 October 1920, 573.
54. Perry, *Belle Moskowitz,* 195.
55. Barnard, "The Woman Voter Gains Power," 20.

bility for women's votes and women's issues, and many rank-and-file women joined all-female Republican or Democratic clubs, which discussed issues, had speakers and may have provided the "feeling of party participation without the substance of such participation."[56] The existence of separate women's organizations in both parties and at both state and national levels has been a source of controversy ever since the 1920s. Some women activists immediately questioned the need for "Women's Divisions" (and indeed for the fifty-fifty plans) on grounds that they perpetuated the notions that political women were significantly different than political men. Nonetheless, separate women's organizations within both parties persisted, even as increasing numbers of women ascended the "male" pathways to party and political power.

The justification for the special places for women within partisan politics was based on an understanding of gender differences that was widely, though not universally, accepted by both men and women. There were two forms of this argument. One was essentially a socialization argument, while the other rested on the notion of "separate spheres" or innate gender differences. The former argument was framed in terms of men's and women's different experiences, or more specifically women's lack of experience with partisan politics. "Why Outside?" asked an article with this title in the *Woman Citizen* in 1922. The author argued that women were still outside the inner party councils because they had not yet developed a good sense of politics. "The nonchalance and assurance with which the men ignore the women until the matters really affecting party business and policy have been attended to reveal perfect confidence in the impotency of the feminine phalanx. When a belated attention is granted, an empty form of recognition is bestowed and encouragement is given in some harmless plan of activity."[57] Even in the mid-40s, when Marguerite Fisher surveyed national committeewomen from both parties, one respondent said despairingly, "Women are still on the outside looking in." It should be noted, however, that two-thirds of the committeewomen did believe that they had genuine political influence.[58]

56. Taylor, *Women's Entry into Party Politics*, 246.
57. *Woman Citizen*, 18 November 1922, 17.
58. Fisher, "Women in Party Politics," 88.

It was widely thought and argued that because women had less experience with things political (read "partisan" or "electoral"), they were less loyal to parties, and this could be seen as a negative or a positive attribute depending on the observers. David Lawrence wrote in the *New York Evening World* about women voters' greater "independence of judgment which makes them difficult of control by political machines." Although women have joined parties, "they show little sign of becoming thick and thin party supporters."[59] Disputes within the New Jersey parties occurred because even those women who did become active in the parties tended to be a bit more independent-minded than the parties were used to. Lillian Feickert, the former suffragist who led the women's division of the New Jersey Republican party, frequently said that "We women are for the Republican party right, but not right or wrong."[60] Mary Garrett Hay, urging the Republicans to give women equal representation in party councils, said in 1920 that party leaders "must keep in mind that women are not swayed by party tradition to the extent that men are and will often be found unwilling blindly to follow party dictation. I myself am a strong party woman, but I know from the contacts of my work that the women generally who are entering the electorate this year are not as yet solidified in party molds."[61]

In Illinois, Republican women opposed a machine candidate in the primary; the machine candidate won. "By the code of party ethics," said Winifred Dobyns, the chairman of the Republican Women's Committee of Illinois, "it was my duty as an officer of the party to swallow my disappointment and take up the cudgels for the successful candidate. How could I do so? I had said that I believed him to be totally unfit to hold office. Needless to say, I resigned." Belle Moskowitz, advisor to Al Smith and certainly one of the most politically powerful women in the 1920s, said that parties had not been fully hospitable to women because "the men are not yet sure that women can demonstrate that solidarity which means success at the polls." There is certainly abundant testimony in contemporary periodicals of women's independent behavior within the parties.[62]

59. *Woman Citizen,* 26 August 1922, 1.

60. Gordon, *After Winning,* 87.

61. *New York Times,* 2 June 1920, 3.

62. See Dobyns, "The Lady and the Tiger," 44; Moskowitz quotation is from the *New York Times,* 28 April 1926; see also Taylor, *The Entrance of Women into Party Politics,* 226–30.

The argument that women lacked the political experience to be able to participate fully in the party system was used to support the parties' fifty-fifty plans and other special systems to guarantee women some representation. Emily Newell Blair, a Democratic leader and a thoughtful observer of the entry of women into politics, wrote in 1925 that she could not predict how long these special places for women would be needed. "But as more and more women come to earn places as individuals the special places will probably disappear." She argued that women should not be unhappy that there are "token women" in politics: this "stage-setting" (encouraging what she called "stage women" to enter politics) "serves to encourage women to come into partisan politics. The politicians want them inside badly enough to offer them inducements—not because they love them inside but because they fear them outside. On the woman's part, too, it is a practical proposition. With the exception of the wives and a few lawyers and professional women, it is the only way they could get into partisan politics. And they know it and welcome it."[63]

The second form of the argument against women's full participation rested on assumptions about innate gender differences. William Allen White, Kansas gubernatorial candidate, remarked in 1924 that "woman's place in politics is about four feet from the kitchen sink," and although a subsequent article in the *New York Times* asserted that his were not commonly held views, when he expanded his remarks his position does not seem too distant from many men (and some women) in the 1920s. "There are plenty of good causes in politics . . . special causes, tragic needs where women as women are demanded by the cruel injunctions of a man-made world. But when a woman gets outside of that area— her own natural ground—she is a nuisance. I suppose if a woman wants to be a convention delegate or a county, state or national committeewoman, that's her business. But being in politics, she should, as far as she can, keep her interests centered on things of the home and her fundamental duties assigned to her by nature."[64]

This argument also reflects the persistence of the view that politics is exclusively partisan and therefore male. Whatever organiza-

63. Blair, "Men in Politics as a Woman Sees Them" 513–22.
64. *New York Times*, 4 January 1925, sec. 8, p. 2.

tional skills and resources women possessed were by definition not political skills. Ruth McCormick, in a 1920 speech to Republican men, said, "I doubt sometimes if you quite realize how experienced we are both in organization and in politics . . . you will forgive us then, if we smile at times today when on occasions our men colleagues on the party Committees serving with us whisper that in time we will learn the political game, but we must have patience! I wonder, if they think at all, how they think we became enfranchised."[65]

Nonetheless she also recognized that the cultural connotations of "politics" operated to distance many women. She went so far as to claim that "the presence of so few women in active politics is due not so much to men's great reluctance to admit them as to women's great indifference to being admitted. Too many women mouth the phrase 'going into politics' as if it were either dangerous or corrupt. Yet women cannot separate politics from civic life and expect to advance that civic life."[66]

DISILLUSIONMENT

There was a general sense that by the late 1920s, women's political influence within the parties had declined. Anna Harvey's recent research provides another account of both this widely shared perception and the eventual disillusionment of women activists such as Blair. Harvey examines the political and organizational response of the Republicans to women voters and finds that, in private correspondence, Republican leaders took seriously what they perceived to be women's particular interests, and engaged in symbolic politics (such as a "Social Justice Day" in October of 1920, to which delegations of women from around the country were invited) designed to appeal to those interests.[67] And, as noted above, Republican party organizations were re-formed and expanded to include women. At the same time, Republican leaders including Harding, Coolidge, and RNC Chairman William Hays were "engaged in a remarkably unanimous and seemingly contradictory effort to de-

65. Miller, *Ruth Hanna McCormick,* 129.
66. *Ibid.,* 189.
67. Harvey, "Uncertain Victory," 16–18.

emphasize the political relevance of gender." Harvey explains this apparent contradiction:

> Republican leaders were effectively asserting that gender was a natural and cultural, but not a political phenomenon. Women were "different" from men, and it was therefore electorally beneficial to the Republican party to segregate women organizationally, as female party workers would communicate better with potential female Republicans than would men. . . . But Republican leaders were also careful publicly to deny the political relevance of gender, implying that women did not require *representation* as women. That is, the "interests" of women (in the home, in children, in other women) were presented by these elites as "natural" tendencies of women which might influence the way in which they considered the issues presented to them, not political demands which required representation in policy.[68]

In 1920, Will Hays said, in a speech to midwestern Republican women leaders who were demanding equal representation, "The Republican Party offers the women everything we offer the men. Republican women come into the party not as women, but as voters entitled to participate and participating as other voters. They are not to be separated or segregated, but assimilated and amalgamated."[69]

Republican women leaders often went along with the argument that gender differences were natural but should not require political responses. In 1927 Mrs. Sallie Hert, vice chairman of the RNC, held a three day session to "perfect party organization among women." She urged the women to "advise [the men] when our experiences can contribute to their work. Factions between men and women defeat our party purposes as much as factions between the women. . . . Organize, work, build permanently, and don't complain to the men."[70]

Similarly, the Democratic party took pains to connect the party's

68. Harvey, "Uncertain Victory," 21.
69. *New York Times*, 6 January 1920, 1.
70. *New York Times*, 13 January 1927, 3.

stands on campaign issues to women's presumed agenda. In 1924, for example, the DNC produced the *Women's Democratic Campaign Manual,* in which the major issues are presented and then put in the context of women's presumed interests in "housekeeping" (in the broadest sense) and in protecting the interests of future generations. Conservation (protection of public lands) is important because women realize "what it will mean to future generations to have their share of our country's riches descend to them uncontrolled by selfish monopoly and unspoiled by the present needless waste." The "Republican tariffs" are described as the cause of the high cost of living, of particular concern to women who "buy or influence the buying of practically all that the [25 million] families require in the way of food, clothing, furnishings, and the scores of other items of necessity, culture, comfort and health." The effects of specific tariffs on such things as buttons, gloves, linens, salt and sugar are then described.[71] At the same time, party leaders, male and female, were emphatic about the amalgamation of women into the party. They objected to women's organizations that were not part of the party hierarchy. When the formation of an organization called Women Democrats of America was proposed (apparently with the support of Tammany), for example, Mrs. Bass said "we suffrage women worked for fifty years to get the ballot so that we might work with the men. I take particular pride that in the Democratic national organization the men have taken us into equal partnership. Our conviction is against women getting together on a sex basis."[72]

The notion that women exercised their citizenship in an indirect and disinterested manner allowed male party leaders to distinguish them from other social groups (such as farmers, manufacturers, immigrants, or southerners, for example). Party politics had traditionally been based on political favors and quid pro quo relationships that allowed the parties to respond, on some level, at least, to a variety of demands by groups. But the fact that women customarily framed their positions in terms of public-spirited civic virtue encouraged party leaders to see women as bringing an alternative

71. Democratic National Committee, *Women's Democratic Campaign Manual* (Washington, D.C., 1924), 34, 37.

72. *New York Times,* 5 February 1920, 8.

perspective into politics, rather than as bringing a new set of demands into politics. Thus at the same time that women's policy agenda was losing momentum in the late 1920s, the discourse within the parties became somewhat broader, relying less exclusively on the reciprocal bargaining of constituent groups and including more of the traditionally feminine concerns about public welfare and social justice. Essentially, I am arguing that when the very male world of party politics opened slightly to include women, it brought in many of women's traditional policy concerns and women's ways of considering policy alternatives, while at the same time denying that these were women's special interests (in the same way that, say, midwestern farmers had a special interest in government funding of railroads or highways). For example, local party organizations had initially resisted the use of candidate questionnaires and forums, which had been introduced by the LWV as part of what Emily Newell Blair called women's "program method" for political campaigns and voter education. But by the end of the 1920s the local party organizations had become more comfortable with this approach.

Such changes in the way parties operated and the way politics was conceived, however, are apparent mostly in hindsight. At the time it simply appeared to women (and correctly) that they were unable to secure much power within the parties. Male leaders responded to women's concerns on a primarily symbolic basis, which essentially left women without the resources they needed to establish themselves firmly within the party councils; such a response was possible because the men controlled the nomination and elections processes within the parties. Despite the spread of the fifty-fifty rules, it was widely felt that independent-minded and feminist women were less likely to be elected or appointed by the late 1920s. In 1920, when the Democratic State Executive Committee of Tennessee created a sort of adjunct committee of twenty women who were to be members of the state Democratic Committee, they asked the Tennessee Woman Suffrage Association to name the twenty women.[73] As the decade wore on, however, Emily Newell Blair claimed that "the kind of woman who could or would

73. *Woman Citizen*, 24 April 1920, 1178.

4.2 Newspaper Coverage of Women and Politics, 1916–1932

	Number of Articles				
	1916	1920	1924	1928	1932
Democratic Party°	0	46	95	20	15
Republican Party°	0	75	105	16	9
Presidential Campaign	0	3	48	141	6
Politics	9	23	89	46	19
Suffrage	236	481	2	3	0

Source: New York Times Index for 1916, 1920, 1924, 1928, and 1932.
° Includes articles referring to women at the national conventions and women's relations with the presidential candidates.

urge her state's member on a Resolutions Committee to vote for
a measure which she thought was based on women's values, who
could sway delegates at a convention, has all too often been succeeded by the wife of some officeholder whose aim in politics is
to help him to success, or a woman who follows instructions from
some men in order to advance herself to office."[74]

This seemed to be true in many places. In Connecticut, Republican machine politicians "refused to grant women decision-making
roles on their party committees. They gave official status to more
conservative women—those who had never been active suffragists
or even leading anti-suffragists."[75]

An analysis of the *New York Times Index* for the presidential
election years of 1916 through 1932, presented in Table 4.2, further
supports the idea that perceptions of women as having an independent and thus interesting political status declined sharply in the
late 1920s. The high incidence of articles about women in the
parties in 1920 and 1924 reflects the high level of fairly public
conflict (described above) between men in the parties and women
demanding organizational changes. This focus for news articles
nearly disappeared in 1928 and 1932. In the 1928 election, which
gave a high profile to "women's issues," expectations about
women's votes and the widespread participation of women in the
campaign produced 141 articles that related to women and the
presidential race. By 1932, coverage of women in the parties or

74. Emily Newell Blair, "Why I Am Discouraged About Women in Politics,"
Woman's Journal (January 1931), 20–22.
75. Nichols, *Votes and More for Women*, 52.

in the campaign was minimal. To some extent this reflects the overwhelming focus on issues associated with the Depression; and it indicates that the presence of women in electoral and party politics was no longer a novelty. But this finding suggests that the process of redrawing the gendered boundaries within the parties and party politics had been pretty much completed by 1932 (in the same vein, the *Woman Citizen* ceased publication in 1931). These boundaries would not really be subject to renegotiation until the 1970s.

This kind of change obviously represented a narrowing of opportunities for women and was seen as such by many women in politics at the time. Emily Newell Blair, for example, argued in the mid-1920s that the impact of women in politics was being assessed according to the false expectations raised by people who were "reformers first and suffragists only as a means." If the early suffragists, who wanted the vote as a matter of simple justice, were able to evaluate women's progress since the ratification of the Nineteenth Amendment, they would come to quite a different judgment. "Two women Governors of States! They would pounce upon this fact with joy . . . ; for setting that fact against the intermingled dismay and fury such a situation would have caused in their day, they would realize, as we do not, that it indicates a change in the whole attitude of society."[76] With a similarly optimistic perspective, she pointed out that for women to achieve more progress in gaining political office, recruitment pools would have to grow larger: women would need to serve at the level of local and state offices, so that they could build up the political capital to run for Congress. By 1930, however, Blair was disillusioned. Though still a loyal Democrat who would receive several appointments at the federal level during the Roosevelt administration, Blair felt that in playing the "man's game" of partisan politics, women had "lost their strategic position." This was true because women had not voted to support women candidates, and the strongest, most independent women were no longer elected and appointed to office. Though she never supported the organization of a separate woman's party (as another Democratic politician,

76. Blair, "Are Women a Failure in Politics?" 516.

Anne Martin, eventually did), she concluded that she had, in fact, been somewhat deluded into thinking that women could make many gains through traditional party politics. "[O]nly as we organize as women, work as women and stand behind women, not only in politics but everywhere, will we make ourselves a real force."[77] At about the same time, Eleanor Roosevelt, also decrying a separate women's party, advocated the selection and backing of women bosses by women voters. Women should organize within parties, in districts, counties and states, to pick efficient leaders "whom we will support and by whose decisions we will abide. With the power of unified women voters behind them, such women bosses would be in a position to talk in terms of 'business' with the men leaders."[78]

The story of women's involvement in the Democratic and Republican parties in the 1920s can be understood by thinking in terms of a struggle to redefine boundaries. Before 1920, party politics was effectively a male domain, and because party politics defined politics for most Americans, women like Carrie Chapman Catt knew that women had to enter this domain in order to be effective politically. Because votes (along with money) were the primary resources by which party elites built and maintained their power, the potential power of women's votes was sufficient to put organizational change on the agenda. Nonetheless the equal representation of men and women at all levels of party organization was not implemented easily or uniformly, and the little research that does exist suggests that these changes came about through a process of demand, negotiation, and compromise in which women with solid power bases were most likely to triumph in their dealings with the male-controlled party organizations. At the level of grass-roots party organization, women came into the parties quickly and stayed. Even as early as 1920, Mary Garrett Hay claimed that the Republicans had 1700 women acting as county leaders or co-

77. Emily Newell Blair, "Wanted—A New Feminism," *Independent Woman* (December 1930), 544; and see Estelle B. Freedman, "Separatism as Strategy: Female Institution Building and American Feminism, 1870–1930," *Feminist Studies* 5 (1979), 512–29.

78. *New York Times*, 10 March 1928, 3.

leaders, and 30,000 precinct leaders. In 1924, Emily Newell Blair recounted how, when she revived the Women's Bureau again in 1922, "an enormous correspondence sprung up almost overnight. It appeared that women had only been waiting for a chance at Democratic headquarters. Our personal mail has averaged 1500 letters a month, a total of 25,000 letters."[79] It is certainly clear that the image of parties had changed by the 1928 elections: the idea of women as canvassers, telephoners, campaign aides, convention speakers, poll watchers and election officials was now an accepted part of American politics. For good or ill, the nation became more used to the idea of women being involved as campaign workers, party officials and, at times, as candidates. A journalist who traveled the country in 1928 interviewing party leaders commented on the "invasion" of female "politicos": "Gone is the last safely masculine sport, saving looking for new polar lands."[80]

For most women who were partisan activists, the fact that they had been invited in this far was sufficient. For those who, like Emily Newell Blair or Eleanor Roosevelt, had hoped for a more substantial change in both practices and policies, their perception that the boundary had simply been re-established around women's special place within the parties produced disappointment and anger. Although the acceptance of the renegotiated boundaries (about which more will be said in the following chapter) indicated the persistence of a "female consciousness" (the notion that women in politics *were* different, for example more altruistic, than men), the arguments of Blair, Roosevelt, Anne Martin and others show a growing feminist consciousness.

79. *Proceedings of the Democratic National Convention* [including Democratic National Committee] 1924, 1098.
80. McCormick, "Enter Women, the New Boss of Politics," 3.

"From Force of Habit She Will Clean This Up"
(Originally from *Judge*, 8 February 1913.)

FIVE   Women as Candidates
              and Officeholders

W^e women must not delude ourselves by thinking we are
politicians, because, with rare exceptions, men with their
longer training have so much greater experience they can always
outdistance us in political strategy. The cheap politician works
for small politics and personal advantage. Our aim should be efficiency in government. We must play a woman's part, think
clearly, look unpleasant facts squarely in the face, and persist in
fundamentally constructive work.

Lucy K. Miller in *The Woman Citizen*, 18 June 1921.

T he idea that women would run for and occupy political
offices in large numbers was not a primary focus of arguments for and against women's suffrage. In a recent book
on women and elective office, R. Darcy, Susan Welch, and Janet
Clark found that "in examining the thinking of the political theo-
rists, the historical background of our present political system, and
the female suffrage movement . . . the idea that women would hold
public office in any large numbers was simply not contemplated or
envisioned." Nancy Cott concurs, saying that suffragists "rarely"
addressed the issue of "whether electing women to high office was
a priority." It is certainly true that putting women in elective office
was not a central goal of the suffrage movement; an article in the
Woman Citizen in 1919 assured readers that though some suffrage
leaders had been proposed for high political office, "most of them
have no wish for anything of the sort."[1]

But as this last quotation indicates, suffragists did sometimes discuss the possibilities of women entering electoral politics as candi-

1. R. Darcy, Susan Welch and Janet Clark, *Women, Elections and Representation*
(New York: Longman, 1987), 2; Cott, *The Grounding of Modern Feminism*, 100;
Woman Citizen, 2 August 1919, 210.

dates. At a suffrage meeting in 1912, Fola LaFollette talked at length about the charge that "Women would take [public] offices from the men." "To oppose women's enfranchisement on the ground that if women vote they will take the offices from the men indicates one of two points of view," she said. "First, either a belief that all women are inferior to men in administrative efficiency and that the community will suffer where they serve; or, second, a belief that, though some women may be the equals or superiors of men in administrative efficiency in certain public capacities, public office is a political plum garden where you wish to maintain a sweet male monopoly at whatever cost to the community." The second attitude, LaFollette believed, was held only by corrupt politicians, and in response to the first position she pointed out that there were already a number of female public officials. Finally, she concluded, even if equal suffrage brought women into the state and national legislatures, this would simply make for better legislation, especially because the interests of women and children will be better represented.[2] Another suffragist wrote in 1917, "We must continually urge a reminder of the fact that the right to vote means the right to be voted for."[3] Breckinridge describes three arguments used "in the days of the suffrage struggle" regarding women and public employment. One argument held that there were some offices for which women were especially suited (e.g., judgeships in juvenile courts); another "supported the admission of women to legislative bodies for the same reason"; and a third argued that this was simply one more way of increasing women's occupational opportunities.[4] And it was certainly the case that during the 1920s women did run for office in increasing numbers, and this trend was intensively examined, commented on, and enjoyed by politically active women and women writers, particularly in the pages of the *Woman Citizen*.

During the late nineteenth and early twentieth centuries, women ran for and won office in both suffrage and non-suffrage

2. National American Woman Suffrage Association, *Twenty-Five Answers to Antis* (Five-minute speeches delivered at a meeting on 11 March 1912, at the Metropolitan Temple in New York City and later published as a booklet), 13–14.

3. Katherine Grinnell, *Women's Place in Government* (New York: Bickerdike and Winegard, 1917), 5–6.

4. Breckinridge, *Women in the Twentieth Century*, 295.

states, though these offices were almost uniformly related to the governance of school systems. In the 1860s and 1870s, for example, a few women were elected to Massachusetts school committees even though women could not vote in their elections, and in 1906 eighteen women were elected county school superintendents (out of fifty-three) in South Dakota.[5] And of course some women had been appointed to public office before 1920, usually to boards of state charities, health boards, or correctional institutions.[6]

WOMEN IN CONGRESS

Previous to the ratification of the Nineteenth Amendment, Jeannette Rankin of Montana was the only woman who had served in the U.S. Congress. Elected in 1916, she served only two years, then ran unsuccessfully for the Senate (she was again elected to the House in the early 1940s). In a truly ironic twist, the first woman to sit in the House of Representatives after women all over the country were enfranchised was an anti-suffragist, Alice Robertson of Oklahoma, who failed to win re-election in 1922.

Of the handful of women who held seats in the House of Representatives in the decade after suffrage, most were widows who were initially appointed to complete their deceased husbands' unexpired terms.[7] A few—notably Democrat Mary Norton of New Jersey, Republican Ruth Baker Pratt (the first woman to serve as a New York City alderman), and Ruth Hanna McCormick, a Republican from Illinois—could be considered politicians in their own right. By the end of the decade what was at first the startling spectacle of women in the halls of Congress had assumed some familiarity: a 1929 article asserted that "It is probable that women's membership in the legislative assembly of the nation has been established as a permanent feature of our national life. . . . There can hardly be any further novelty in such membership."[8]

5. Sumner, *Equal Suffrage,* 128.

6. Breckinridge, "The Activities of Women Outside the Home," 743.

7. This was a custom that persisted until fairly recently. By 1969, sixty-six women had served in the House of Representatives, of whom twenty-nine had been widows of congressmen. Frieda L. Gehlen, "Women Members of Congress: A Distinctive Role," in *A Portrait of Marginality,* ed. Marianne Githens and Jewel L. Prestage (New York: David McKay, 1977), 308.

8. George E. Anderson, "Women in Congress," *The Commonweal* 9 (13 March 1929), 534.

While only seven women ran for Congress in 1920, approximately twenty women were nominated to run for House seats in each subsequent election year during the 1920s; in 1922 six women were also nominated for Senate seats, making that year the numerical peak for women candidates (twenty-eight). Some of the women who were first appointed to fill out their husbands' terms (Edith Nourse Rogers, for example) continued to run successfully as incumbents. But the majority of the women who ran for congressional office were "sacrificial lambs," nominated by the states or district's minority party. In 1922, for example, five Republican women candidates included four in Democratic districts (the other won her race); the ten Democratic women candidates were from predominantly Republican districts; and the other nominees included women from the Prohibition, Socialist, and Farmer-Labor parties.[9] An editorial in *The Woman Citizen* concluded that "First of all it is clear that the barriers in the way of women being elected to any political office are almost insurmountable. The dominant political parties do not nominate women for political office if there is a real chance for winning. Political offices are the assets of the political machine. In general, they are too valuable to be given to women. They are used to pay political debts or to strengthen the party, and so far the parties are not greatly in debt to women, and it has not been shown that it strengthens a party to nominate them."[10]

WOMEN GOVERNORS AND
STATE OFFICERS

During the 1920s there were two highly publicized women governors, both wives of men who had served as governor. Nellie Tayloe Ross took office as governor of Wyoming in January of 1925 (her husband, the governor, had died less than three months before). "Ma" Ferguson in Texas was elected as a sort of stand-in for her husband, the former governor who had been impeached and was thus ineligible to run.[11]

9. See Breckinridge, *Women in the Twentieth Century*, 301–5.
10. *Woman Citizen*, 18 November 1922.
11. Mrs. Ross served only one term and lost her bid for re-election. Mrs. Ferguson was not renominated by the Democrats in 1926, but did serve again as governor in the thirties.

Across the East, Midwest and West, a number of women were appointed or elected to statewide office. In New Mexico in 1920, the governor appointed both Hispanic and Anglo women to every state board, a woman became assistant secretary of state, and women moved into control of the public welfare board.[12] Two years later a Hispanic Democratic woman was elected secretary of state, and an Anglo Democratic woman was elected state superintendent of public instruction. Both of these positions fairly quickly became "traditional" women's offices—a good example of a situation where the boundary delineating appropriate political positions for men and women was redefined during this period. In fact, by 1930 thirteen women across the country had held the position of secretary of state (a few appointed, most elected), and ten states had women state superintendents of public instruction during the twenties (a few states, almost all in the West, had elected women to this post repeatedly). In contrast, by 1930 no woman had served as a state attorney general.[13]

By 1929, the *New York Times* reported a number of women in state offices: two state treasurers, a secretary of state (Gladys Pyle, a Republican who was re-elected secretary of state in South Dakota, and who led her ticket and received the greatest number of votes ever cast for a constitutional officer in South Dakota), three state superintendents of public instruction, a (re-elected) state auditor, one elected member of a state railroad commission, and Florence Allen, who was re-elected to her second six-year term on the Ohio Supreme Court. In fact, though Ohio voted for Hoover by a 700,000 majority and for the Republican gubernatorial candidate by 270,000, Judge Allen (running on a nonpartisan judicial ballot) received 953,512 votes, over 350,000 more than her nearest opponent. Additionally Breckinridge reported that during the 1920s four women were chosen clerks of their state Supreme Courts, one woman succeeded another as elected reporter of the Indiana Supreme Court, and Mrs. Esther Andrews of Massachusetts served several terms as one of eight "governor's councilors," with "power over appointments, clemency, expenditures and other aspects of state administration." A survey conducted by the

12. Jensen, "Disfranchisement is a Disgrace," 25.
13. Breckinridge, *Women in the Twentieth Century*, 317–21.

5.1 Women Serving in State Legislatures in the 1920s

Year	Number of Women	Number of States
1921	37	26
1923	98	35
1925	141	38
1927	127	36
1929	149	38
1931	146	39

Source: Breckinridge, *Women in the Twentieth Century,* 322–26.

Woman's Bureau in 1928 and reported in the *New York Times* "reveals that more than 1,000 women have been appointed or elected to State offices throughout the country."[14]

WOMEN STATE LEGISLATORS

Though women had occasionally served in state legislatures before the suffrage amendment was ratified (woman members introduced the ratification resolution in a few states), the number of women running for and achieving state legislative seats increased dramatically during the 1920s. Table 5.1 illustrates this trend.[15]

By 1931 only Louisiana had never elected a female legislator. The first African-American woman to serve in a state legislature, Mrs. E. Howard Harper of West Virginia, had been appointed to succeed her late husband in 1928. The New England and western states led in the number of women elected to legislative and other office; by 1931, for example, Connecticut had elected forty-seven women to statewide office. New Hampshire's legislature included three women in 1921 and 1923, fourteen in 1925, seventeen in 1931, and twenty-four by 1939. Over 320 women had served in state legislatures by the time Breckinridge conducted her study in 1933. The southern states lagged far behind in the extent to which women ran for and won legislative office. In Alabama, for example, one woman served in the state legislature in 1923, another in 1948,

14. Ida Clyde Clark, "Feminists Made Gains in Many Fields in 1928," *New York Times,* 17 February 1929, 8; Breckinridge, *Women in the Twentieth Century,* 318; *New York Times,* 17 February 1929, 8.

15. In 1927, the party breakdown for women legislators was 70% Republican, 25% Democratic, and 4% independent or nonpartisan. Dorothy Moncure, "Women in Political Life," *Current History* 29 (January 1929), 640.

then none until the 1970s and 1980s opened up new possibilities for women in politics. With some fluctuations, the number of women in state offices continued to increase slowly. By 1946 there were 234 women in state legislatures in thirty-nine states and more than 1,500 women in executive positions in state government.[16]

No easily available record exists of the number of women who *ran* for state legislative seats during this time, though the *Woman Citizen* attempted to list all female candidates at least during the mid-1920s. In November of 1922, for example, it surveyed all states for names of women candidates for state and national office; thirty-seven states responded, and these listed 179 female nominees for state legislative seats (either in the Senate or the House). Projecting the same rate of nomination onto the eleven states that didn't respond (which were not concentrated in any particular region) produces an estimate of 232 legislative candidates in the 1922 elections.

More detailed accounts of candidates and races can be found in some states for some years. Connecticut in 1920 saw thirty-four women running for the Connecticut House of Representatives (twenty-eight Democrats, three Republicans, one Socialist, one Farmer-Labor party member, and one independent). The Republican women all won, while only one Democrat did (the Democrats as a whole only elected thirteen legislators to the 262-member House in 1920). In 1922, twenty-seven women ran and seven were elected (six of them Republicans), all from rural areas and five from "GOP strongholds." Thirty-four women ran for House seats in 1924 and fifteen (all Republicans) were elected. In New Jersey, seven women ran on major party tickets for state and county offices in 1920 and 1921, increasing to thirteen in 1922 and 1923, fifteen in 1924, between seventeen and eighteen for the next three years, and dropping back between thirteen and fifteen through 1931.[17]

WOMEN IN COUNTY AND LOCAL
GOVERNMENT OFFICES

It seems safe to say that county and local government presented fewer barriers to women's participation. For many reasons, women

16. *New York Times*, 20 February 1928, 3; Nichols, *Votes and More for Women*, 48; Florence E. Allen, "Participation of Women in Government," *Annals of the American Academy of Political and Social Science* 251 (May 1947), 94–110.

17. Nichols, *Votes and More for Women*, 47–48; Gordon, *After Winning*, 386.

running for and serving as county commissioners, town councilors, or mayors seemed less threatening to voters and to male political elites than women in Congress or holding high state office. First, involvement in these local offices usually represented a part-time job, relatively near the occupant's home: thus women could more easily meet the obligations that they were perceived to have to their families. Second, the work of county and town governments was more easily seen as an extension of women's housekeeping interests and capabilities. These offices were sometimes nonpartisan, in practice if not legally, which may have made it easier for women with little experience as party activists to run for them; and as Breckinridge pointed out in 1933, "competition for power is not so great in that dark continent of American politics."[18] Finally, as Darcy, Welch and Clark argue, "the style of local government differed from that at other levels. It was voluntary, and decisions were typically reached through consensus rather than conflict. In many ways, the style of village politics was a simple extension of personal relationships rather than the politics we have come to know from experiences at the national or even the state level. Given this style, women could participate in local government without being 'politicians.'"[19]

Sophonisba Breckinridge seemed to affirm this argument when her study of "women outside the home" in 1933 found that "It is in the local jurisdiction that the evidence of women's activity is most conspicuous and there has perhaps been more substantial advance in the local than in any other jurisdictions. There have been women mayors; women have sat on boards of aldermen or city councils; they have been comptrollers and city clerks; and they are on boards of county commissioners. . . . [T]he woman in politics progresses faster at home than in the larger political units. . . ."[20]

Though there are no comprehensive data on the number of women elected to county-level offices during the 1920s, information from state *Blue Books* and from secondary sources can help us to piece together a picture of women's involvement in county government. Table 5.2 displays data from a study conducted by the Leagues

18. Breckinridge, *Women in the Twentieth Century*, 332.
19. Darcy, Welch and Clark, *Women, Elections, and Representation*, 9.
20. Breckinridge, "The Activities of Women Outside the Home," 744.

5.2 Women Elected to Local Offices

Year	Number of Women			
	Connecticut	Michigan	Minnesota	Wisconsin
1925	29			
1926			127	58
1927	67	277	209	64
1929	178	590		158
1930			245	

Source: Breckinridge, *Women in the Twentieth Century,* 335, based on a study by the League of Women Voters. Includes city, town, and county officers.

5.3 Women Elected to County Offices

Year	Number of Women							
	IL	MN	IA	WI	PA	SD	OR	NM
1920		38					28	19
1921	23	40	96	26	12	72		
1927		58						32
1928	39							38
1929		59						
1931			137	75	45		35	35
1933						94		

Source: Blue Books for Illinois, Minnesota, Iowa, Wisconsin, Pennsylvania, South Dakota, and Oregon. For New Mexico, Jensen, " 'Disfranchisement Is a Disgrace.' "

of Women Voters in Minnesota, Wisconsin, Connecticut and Michigan and reported by Breckinridge in 1933. These figures cover elected city, town, and county offices and show an average growth in numbers of 223% over the period covered. Table 5.3 suggests that the major part of this increase in female officeholders came at the town and city level, where the average increase per state is 96%.

The variation in the extent to which women ran for and won office in different states can be seen from these data. Iowa, for example, appears more hospitable to women candidates than Illinois. Three states which are not included in these tables illustrate this variation even more clearly.[21] In Texas in 1930 there were 216 women holding county offices, while Alabama in 1931 reported only 5, and did not elect more than a handful of women to these

21. I included in Table 5.3 only states for which I had data at more than one time point.

offices until the late forties. New Hampshire even by 1935 had only 6 women county officials.[22]

Looking at the offices women held gives us a clear sense of which positions were "acceptable" for women to compete for—in other words, a sense of where the gendered boundary had been redrawn. Women's traditional concern with children and education eased the way for women to serve as education officials. In Colorado, a year after women received suffrage in 1893, a woman was elected state superintendent of public instruction; women held that office continuously at least through the 1930s. In New Mexico, where two women had been elected county school superintendents as early as 1908, the 1920 election saw women running for this office in twenty-one of the twenty-nine counties; they were elected in nineteen. Arizona elected women school superintendents in nine out of twelve counties in 1922; in Colorado women served in fifty of sixty-three counties in 1930. In contrast, in Rhode Island, by 1935–36 only two of thirty-nine school superintendents were women, one of these being one of the few part-time superintendents.[23]

The women officeholders enumerated in Table 5.3 consist mostly of county school superintendents in all states. In Iowa, for example, over half the school superintendents in both 1921 and 1931 were women. During the twenties, women in Iowa made inroads into other county offices: 38% of the county recorders were female in 1921, while 56% were women in 1931. There were also, in the latter year, eleven county auditors, eight court clerks, and six treasurers. In some other states, county treasurer, rather than (or in addition to) school superintendent, quickly came to be seen as a woman's job. Texas recorded 109 women county treasurers in

22. Jane Y. McCallum, "Activities of Women in Texas Politics," in *Texas Democracy: A Centennial History of Politics and Personalities of the Democratic Party 1836–1936*, ed. Frank Adams (Austin: Democratic Historical Association, 1937). Reprinted in A. Elizabeth Taylor, *Citizens at Last: The Woman Suffrage Movement in Texas* (Austin: Ellen C. Temple, 1987), 334; Alabama Secretary of State; New Hampshire *Manual for the General Court*. It should be noted that New Hampshire's ten counties provided fewer chances for women to run for and win office than Alabama's 67 or Texas' 254.

23. Charles E. Merriam, *The American Party System* 8th ed. (New York: Macmillan, 1979), 29; Jensen, "Disfranchisement is a Disgrace," 25; *Woman Citizen*, 2 December 1922, 10; Saint, "Women in the Public Service: General Survey," 53; *Manual for the Use of the Rhode Island General Assembly* 1935.

1930 (and only 47 school superintendents), as well as an assortment of county clerks, tax collectors, tax assessors, constables, justices of the peace and other officials. In Pennsylvania, where there were only a few women holding office at the county level early in the decade (most of whom were jury commissioners and recorders), women had moved into positions as county auditors and poor directors (eleven each) by 1931.[24]

The *Woman Citizen* and other periodicals reported on a number of all-female governments in various small towns in Iowa, Oregon, New York, Wyoming, Ohio, Colorado, North Dakota, and Michigan in the 1920s. In most of these instances, women had organized because the male mayors and councils were thought to have abdicated their responsibility: the town needed cleaning up, either physically or morally. Women frequently surprised the male incumbents, who were sometimes their own husbands, and often served for years once the publicity had died down. Stories of these towns can be found in various magazines and newspapers of the time.[25]

A survey conducted in 1930 in Cleveland found that one state senator from Cuyahoga County, three of sixteen state assembly members, and one of twenty-five city council members (down from three in 1927) were women. They also found women occupying eighty appointive governmental jobs, including the manager of the Cleveland office of the Department of Commerce, women who were state-employed factory and building inspectors, and county-level workers in the tax, health, and pension departments.[26] It is clear even from these rather fragmentary data that local government was rapidly opening up to women during the 1920s.

24. Jane Y. McCallum, "Activities of Women in Texas Politics," in *Texas Democracy: A Centennial History of Politics and Personalities of the Democratic Party, 1836–1936*, ed. Frank Adams (Austin: Democratic Historical Association, 1937). Reprinted in *Citizens at Last: The Woman Suffrage Movement in Texas*, ed. Elizabeth A. Taylor (Austin: Ellen C. Temple, 1987); *The Pennsylvania Manual.*

25. *Woman Citizen*, 26 June 1920, 104–5; *Woman Citizen*, 22 April 1922; *Literary Digest*, 4 December 1920, 52; *Literary Digest*, 21 June 1924, 50. Some of these stories are collected in Mildred Adams, "What Are Women Mayors Doing?" *American City* 26 (June 1922), 543–44; Martin Gruberg, *Women in American Politics* (Oshkosh, WI: Academia Press, 1968). 201–3; and Breckinridge, *Women in the Twentieth Century*, 332.

26. Randolph Huus, "Cleveland Women in Government and Allied Fields," *National Municipal Review* 19 (1930), 88–92.

RESISTANCE TO CHANGE

Before women could run for public office, in many cases they had to confront legal barriers; before they could win office, they always had to confront skeptical if not hostile voters, both male and female. In the years before suffrage some assumed, and others feared, that having the vote would automatically give women the right to hold public office. After suffrage this belief persisted among some women. Anna Dickie Olesen, a Senate candidate in Minnesota, said that she had "no apology to make for being a candidate for United States Senator. The highest legal authority in the land gave me the right to vote and therefore to run for office."[27] Political parties, anxious to appeal to women voters, also appeared to support this argument. As soon as the Nineteenth Amendment had been ratified, or even before, political parties in various states formulated plans to nominate women for political offices as a way of attracting women. Just as quickly, their actions were challenged.

Missouri Attorney General Frank McAllister ruled in 1920 that the four women who were candidates for the state legislature were not qualified to serve. "The Missouri law requires that to be a member of the state legislature one must be a male voter and a voter for two years before the election." The women, he ruled, failed on both counts. A Missouri newspaper editorialized that it would be "imprudent" (not wrong!) to exclude women from the "privilege" of holding office.[28] Similarly, the Arkansas attorney general ruled that women were not eligible to hold office, and based on this opinion the secretary of state refused to accept the certification of a woman as a Republican candidate for state superintendent of public instruction.[29] The New Hampshire Supreme Court held that women were eligible since suffrage to hold all elective offices but that the common law made them "ineligible to all others" (i.e., appointive office); at issue here was an appointment of a woman as justice of the peace.[30] Wis-

27. *Woman Citizen*, 2 December 1922, 12.

28. *Woman Citizen*, 30 October 1920, 598.

29. *Woman Citizen*, 30 October 1920, 607.

30. CJD, "The Nineteenth Amendment As Affecting the Right of Women to Hold Public Office," *Temple Law Quarterly* 2 (April 1928), 278–79. Perhaps the clearest statement of the position that women were by nature unsuited for public office can be found in a petition filed in Michigan, where a woman Justice of the Peace required a man to appear before her in regard to the non-payment of a loan. Through his lawyer the man sought a writ to prohibit the woman (Mrs. Patterson) from holding office, "she being a married woman, the wife of Patterson . . . to

consin, which passed an equal rights law in 1921, made sure to mention women's right to hold office: "Women shall have the same rights and privileges under the law as men in the exercise of suffrage, freedom of contract, choice of residence for voting purposes, jury service, and holding office. . . ."[31]

New Mexico's state constitution of 1910 had given women the right to hold office as school superintendents or members of boards of education, but restricted the right of women to vote for these officials: if a majority of voters presented a petition to the county asking that women be disenfranchised, a counter-petition restoring the franchise had to be approved before women could vote again. The constitution was finally altered in 1921 to allow women to hold all offices.[32] Iowa amended its constitution in 1926 by eliminating the word "male" as a qualification for office, and other states did the same in the 1920s, often in response to lobbying by the League of Women Voters and other women's organizations. It was not until 1942, however, that Oklahoma amended its constitution to allow women to hold high state offices; in referenda held in 1923, 1930, and 1935 voters failed to acknowledge the right of women to hold major state offices. Even in 1935, the vote against women garnered a hefty 57% of the vote.[33]

Custom and political parties' desire to ingratiate themselves with women voters often appeared to outweigh legal strictures. The Massachusetts attorney general, like the attorneys general in Oklahoma, Missouri, Arkansas and others states, ruled in 1920 that women were not eligible to hold office. It was pointed out, however, that women had been nominated for office by the Socialist party since 1900; subsequently in the 1920 election the Democrats nominated a woman for state treasurer with no protest from any quarter.[34] At any rate,

---

whom her services as a matter of law belong; and who is legally and presumptively entitled to exercise a coercive influence over her. And a woman by law not being permitted to exercise a judicial office and to discharge the duties thereof, she being sexually unable to do so as a matter of nature and as a matter of law." A circuit court judge dismissed the case on the grounds that the Nineteenth Amendment *did* also confer the right to hold office. *Woman Citizen*, 8 January 1921, 865.

31. Mabel Search, "Women's Rights in Wisconsin," *Marquette Law Review* 6 (1922), 164–69.

32. *Women Citizen*, 7 October 1922; Jensen, "Disfranchisement is a Disgrace."

33. Gruberg, *Women in American Politics*, 169; *Literary Digest*, 5 October 1935, 7; Merriam, *The American Party System*, 30.

34. *Woman Citizen*, 18 December 1920.

references to controversies surrounding women's right to hold office declined rapidly after the initial flurry in 1920 and 1921.

Once women were nominated, most of them had an extremely difficult time winning elections. The *Woman Citizen* provided the most systematic and wide ranging look at the successes and failures of women candidates. When women candidates were surveyed, the magazine asked them to suggest the reasons behind their wins or losses. While a "rich variety" of reasons were given, including minority-party status, "Repeatedly the women say that they had a handicap to overcome in being women." For instance, Lillie M. Tweedy said she failed to be elected to the Indiana Senate because "first, I ran on a Democratic ticket in a very strong Republican county. Second, I am a woman: and there is still much prejudice among men against the women voting and especially holding office as also among women. . . . and I was too liberal toward members of other parties to please altogether our central committee."[35] And Mrs. Elwood S. Sharp, a candidate for the Kansas legislature, commented, "No woman had ever been elected from the district, and so many men were dubious about the wisdom of such a progressive step." Though many women were nominated by the minority party and had little hope of winning, there were exceptions. Two of these were congressional candidates Winifred Lufkin and Helen Statler, both nominated by Republicans in Republican districts, in Massachusetts and Michigan respectively. Both lost in the 1920 election, "showing clearly enough," the *Woman Citizen* believed, "that the rank and file of the men voters of their own party preferred a Democratic male representative in Congress to a woman of their own party."[36] Opposition to a woman "getting a man's salary" was said to figure prominently in the defeat of a Westchester County, New York woman who ran for juvenile court judge.[37]

When Ruth Hanna McCormick ran for congressman-at-large from Illinois in 1928, she was "surprised by the vehemence of resistance to her candidacy because she was a woman." In a typical letter, one man told her, "I would not think of voting for a woman for Congressman-at-Large any more than to vote for one of my cows for such

35. *Woman Citizen*, 2 December 1922, 11.
36. *Woman Citizen*, 13 November 1920, 654.
37. *Woman Citizen*, 8 November 1921.

a responsible office." Even her friends were reluctant to back her, because they thought she did not have a chance to win.[38]

Later, when she had won the Republican nomination for Senator, many pundits and politicians were alarmed at the idea of a woman in the Senate, despite the fact that a number of women had served regularly in the House of Representatives, including eight in the 1929–31 term. Hiram Johnson, Teddy Roosevelt's running mate in 1912, wrote that "Some of us consider it a punch in the eye to the Senate, because [McCormick's primary victory] means the admission of the first woman. It is quite true that the Senate may not have lived up to its traditions of late years, but its thorough breakdown and demoralization, in my opinion, will come with the admission of the other sex."[39] Similarly, a Wisconsin state senator wrote to a local newspaper about his concern that men would not go to the polls "if the Women get Elected to any State Legislature." He feared women's "hair pulling" in the legislature, and predicted that they might be "worse as the Attorneys at present" in this regard.[40]

Elected women claimed almost universally that the men with whom they served were polite and hospitable. When Breckinridge surveyed state legislators, "most of the writers indicated that their legislative experience was an interesting and happy one." At the same time, many of them perceived that women were being used as a political work force by male leaders, but were given few positions of power and did not yet have enough political skills and clout to secure those positions themselves.[41] And there were certainly instances of outright discrimination. In 1923 Miss Amy Wren, the Republican co-leader of the First Assembly District in Brooklyn, resigned the patronage position of deputy attorney general in pro-

38. Miller, *Ruth Hanna McCormick,* 189.

39. Quoted in Miller, *Ruth Hanna McCormick,* 223. This kind of focus on what damage women will do to the institution is similar to the way the issue of women's suffrage in Switzerland was displaced onto an argument about the nature of the formerly all-male cantonal institution (the *Landsgemmeinde*), when the last holdout against woman suffrage was being brought into line with national standards. John Bendix, "Women's Suffrage and Political Culture: A Modern Swiss Case," *Women and Politics* 12 (1992), 27–56.

40. *Woman Citizen,* 28 June 1919, 100.

41. Breckinridge, *Women in the Twentieth Century,* 330–332.

test against the treatment she was accorded: unlike the male deputies, she was put in a crowded room with three stenographers and had to punch a time clock. She was not given a case for which her twenty-three years of legal experience clearly fitted her, and she was paid less than the male deputies.[42]

ESTABLISHING NEW BOUNDARIES

Women did sometimes run difficult, contested campaigns and win, both in general elections and in primaries. Adelina Otero-Warren, for example, who had been school superintendent for Santa Fe County, New Mexico for six years, defeated the incumbent Republican congressman, Nestor Montoya, for the congressional nomination at the 1922 Republican state convention.[43] Nonetheless, as discussed above, it is evident from an unsystematic sampling of information about early women candidates and office holders that women were frequently nominated as "sacrificial lambs," and clearly a large proportion of the major parties' nominations of women did take place in situations where the party was in the minority.

A look at candidates and officeholders in the 1920s can illustrate how the gendered boundary in politics is maintained even as its location shifts. Women are allowed to vote, but perhaps not to run for office. They are allowed to run for office, but are rarely nominated in contests they have a chance of winning. Once in office, they are expected to exhibit certain attributes, including a womanly demeanor, a lack of political ambition, and an interest in women's issues. Women were allowed into politics, in other words, but confined mostly to a clearly bounded area.

If an elected or appointed woman was the first to hold a particular office, a good deal of media attention was focused on her, and how reporters described her tells us something about public perceptions of political women. Especially early in the decade, the media coverage of women holding public office usually followed a standard formula. Articles mentioned the woman's dress, hair, voice, and genteel demeanor, and also mentioned (sometimes sounding somewhat surprised) that she exhibited parliamentary skills, paid attention to speakers, or otherwise comported herself

42. *New York Times,* 21 January 1925, 23.
43. *Woman Citizen,* 7 October 1922.

much like a male politician. The writers seemed to see their task as reassuring their readers both that women could follow the political rules of the game *and* that despite their entry into the male domain of politics, women "remained women."

An article about Mrs. Florence Knapp, who was elected secretary of state for New York in 1924, is a perfect example of this sort of description. "When the new Secretary of State mounted the platform in the Assembly Chamber with Dr. James A. Hamilton, the outgoing Secretary," wrote a reporter for the *New York Times*, "all eyes were focused on her. She wore a peach colored velvet dress and was a picture of loveliness. . . . From the moment she called the assemblage to order until the benediction had been pronounced it was apparent that she was a woman well qualified to preside at a public gathering. Her clear, musical voice carried plainly to all parts of the chamber. She plainly won the hearts of the spectators almost instantly." Mrs. Knapp herself mentioned that she was glad to be accepted by the members of the Assembly and only wanted to demonstrate that she could do a good job as Secretary of State.[44]

Some accounts focused on the woman's political skills, while many went to extreme lengths to attribute traditional womanly characteristics and behavior to female politicians. When Miss Margaret Fort, an assemblywoman from Essex, New Jersey and the daughter of former Governor J. Franklin Fort, occupied the Speaker's chair briefly in the New Jersey Assembly, "She was escorted to the rostrum, received the gavel and presided with all the poise and familiarity with parliamentary routine noted in a veteran speaker."[45] On the other hand, we find in the rotogravure section of the *New York Times* in June 1920, among many pictures taken at the Republican National Convention, one identified as "Mrs. John G. South, of Frankfort, Kentucky, whose smile is said to have won her the chairmanship of the Women's Division of the Republican National Committee"—a claim which is not supported in any other accounts.[46]

Though the *New York Times* was, of course, written and edited almost entirely by males, women observers were equally eager to

44. *New York Times*, 2 January 1925, 3.
45. *New York Times*, 11 February 1924, 28.
46. *New York Times*, 13 June 1920 (III).

reassure their readers of the "womanliness" of women candidates and officeholders. The *Woman Citizen* in 1922 described Dr. Amy Kaukonen, who had just been elected mayor of Fairport, Ohio: "She is small, blonde, attractive, short-skirted, feminine—and altogether one of the finest signs of women's work in municipal housekeeping."[47] Certainly many of the women in politics themselves accepted these gender stereotypes and in any case had to deal with others' widespread acceptance of such stereotypes. Elisabeth Israels Perry, Belle Moskowitz's biographer, describes clearly the ways that Moskowitz was able to preserve her political influence in part *through* her efforts to project a traditional, womanly impression. "Moskowitz was certainly conscious of the risks," says Perry. Early in her partnership with Al Smith "she decided to stay out of the public eye as much as possible. She declined Smith's offers of state government posts, and rarely allowed herself to be quoted directly on Smith's affairs." Before 1928, an observer would have had to be intimately connected with Democratic party politics to realize the extent of her influence. "This tactic not only protected Smith, it was completely consistent with Moskowitz's view of how a woman should function in society."[48] Frances Perkins recalled that she learned early in her political career that men associate women, even political women, with motherhood. "I said to myself, 'That's the way to get things done, I'm sure. So behave, so dress and so comport yourself that you remind them subconsciously of their mothers.'"[49]

One aspect of "how a woman should function in society" had to do with political motivations. As I discussed in chapter 2, it was widely thought and argued, by both men and women, that women entered politics for altruistic reasons or to accomplish certain collective ends, and not to gain a share of the political spoils (the goal that was seen to motivate male politicians). Thus though Belle Moskowitz, for example, had strongly-held policy goals and was "ambitious" for Al Smith, as the passage above implies she herself did not display any political ambition. Moskowitz played the role of a counselor to Smith—he was someone to instruct and de-

47. *Woman Citizen,* 25 March 1922, 19
48. Perry, *Belle Moskowitz,* 151.
49. Wandersee, "Frances Perkins Meets Tammany Hall," 23.

velop—but she played this role unobtrusively, not publicly, as would a male politician with his protégé. "Moskowitz took part in these ["kitchen cabinet"] meetings from the sidelines, plying her knitting needles and speaking only when asked for her views. As a woman, and especially one whose power depended on the continued favor of the man she advised, she knew her place and kept to it." In this way she was able to insert her own views without threatening the men. In addition, she never took advantage of her relationship to Smith by allowing others to use her to advance their own careers. This "established Moskowitz as someone pointedly not engaged in the empire building usually associated with ambitious men."[50] A similar description might be given of Julia Lathrop who, in fact, really was "building an empire." The first head of the Children's Bureau, she "advanced women's influence in government without explicitly challenging women's sphere. . . . Lathrop's emphasis on women's maternal role and her denial of female career ambition allowed the Children's Bureau to extend its influence without appearing to do so."[51] On the other hand, a cautionary tale for ambitious women might be glimpsed in the career of Mabel Walker Willebrandt. Appointed an Assistant Attorney General by Harding in 1921, she focused her ambition on an eventual federal judgeship. During the 1928 election contest she campaigned vigorously (and controversially, alienating "wet" Republicans) for Hoover. Her "fierce drive for success," and her controversial aggressiveness on the campaign trail (*Time* referred to her speeches as having "plenty of stingo") made her "too hot to handle. There would be no judgeship."[52]

A woman Tammany leader told the *New York Times* in 1925 that her entrance into politics had been accidental: at first she had been asked to be a co-leader for a portion of the First Assembly District, as the party created positions for women, and she had refused. "I was absolutely without experience, almost without interest in such things. I had not been a suffragist. No, I had not been an anti either.

50. Perry, *Belle Moskowitz*, 153–155.

51. Ladd-Taylor, "Hull House Goes to Washington," 112.

52. Dorothy M. Brown, "Power in Washington: Networking in the 1920s from Willebrandt to Roosevelt" (paper presented at the Conference on Women, Politics and Change, New School for Social Research, New York, April 1990), 11.

The subject simply had never appealed to me." Nonetheless, she had found her work as co-leader (and as leader when her co-leader died) very satisfying. "I soon found that there was a very real field for a woman in such work." This may sound like ambition, but Mrs. Nolan continues by claiming that women have a particular talent for dealing with other women and with the small, daily problems that people bring to their party leaders.

> There are some things that a woman can understand bet-
> ter than a man. My work, of course, has been largely
> with women, they are more ready to come to a woman
> with their troubles than to a man. And it is from these
> small troubles, which they may think are too small to
> take to a man, that important things develop. But always
> I have consulted with the men and have counted upon
> their advice. It is not the kind of work for a woman to
> do alone. . . . No woman would be capable of running
> this district alone. It is out of the question. . . . I will
> not say . . . that I do not think women are capable of
> holding big political offices. But it is unreasonable to
> think that we women could step in and undertake with
> equal success what men have had ages to learn and to
> fit themselves for. I do think there are many places for
> women in politics, and that it is our duty as well as our
> privilege to do our part. Of course, women ought to be
> trained for such careers. How? In the same way men
> are trained. Study will help to lay the foundation, but
> the rest must come from association with those who
> have already accomplished big things.[53]

In Minnesota in 1920, a woman was elected mayor of a small town and then defeated for re-election two years later. She attributed her defeat in part to her desire to "clean up" the town and in part to the fact that she "didn't fight very hard for election" because she "thought it uncalled for and manlike."[54] Several candidates told the *Woman Citizen* that they had been nominated without their knowl-

53. *New York Times*, 22 February 1925, sec. 8, p. 10.
54. *Woman Citizen*, 8 April 1922, 22.

edge, and even Jessie Hooper, who had been president of the Wisconsin League of Women Voters and was nominated by the Democrats for U.S. Senate (with no chance of winning), said "she would have been no more surprised if she had been asked to join a party to the North Pole."[55] Similarly, Indiana's first woman legislator, Julia Nelson, was "probably more surprised to find herself in the Legislature than anyone in the state," having been nominated two days before the election when the incumbent died.[56]

It was widely believed that women ran for office primarily to raise important issues, not to win. A *New York Times* editorial in 1928 included excerpts from a letter written by a woman who had been defeated in her bid for office. She did not grudge the time or money spent, however: "On the contrary, I feel that the way for us to force the fighting on the things we care about is to get a lot of qualified women and run for office— women who are not afraid—women who don't expect to get elected anyhow and so will not be depressed by defeat—to run on clear-cut issues—on platforms which can be understood."[57]

In general, exhibiting a lack of personal ambition was the rule for women candidates in the 1920s. To the extent that "politician" referred to someone who was personally ambitious and/or sought benefits for himself and his friends, women could be "in politics" but were usually not seen as politicians. When the *Woman Citizen* or other publications interviewed women in office, only a few saw their position as part of a wider personal political strategy. Ruth Averill, elected in 1920 to the Nevada state legislature, for example, was a young law school graduate who said "the experience helped to launch me into the profession which I intend to follow from now on, namely, law." She was unusual in the way she saw politics as part of a career, and did not hesitate to admit it.[58]

As the decade wore on, the media coverage of political women grew somewhat less effusive, more factual, less focused on the fact that they were women and on their "womanly" qualities. For example, a *New York Times* article in 1928 about Lillian Feickert's

55. *Woman Citizen*, 15 July 1922, 6.
56. *Woman Citizen*, 29 January 1929, 931.
57. *New York Times*, 28 August 1928, 22.
58. *Woman Citizen*, 30 July 1921.

decision to seek the Republican nomination for U.S. Senator recounted her history as a suffrage leader, asked her if she was a
"women's candidate" (she said, predictably, that she was not), but
primarily emphasized her political experience, skills, and successes.[59] Similarly, a *Times* article in the following year notes the
election of a Queens woman to the Board of Aldermen. The Republican County Committee from the Fourth Assembly District
gave Mrs. Ebba Winslow eighty-six votes to her male opponents'
fifty-eight, and the news story gives a straightforward account of
this, as well as Winslow's previous experience (which included a
run for the State Assembly, appointment as a deputy sheriff, delegate to the Republican National Convention).[60]

Women candidates, nonetheless, remained keenly conscious that
they were defining new roles for women, pushing the limits of
what was considered expected or acceptable. Jessie Jack Hooper,
a Democratic candidate for the U.S. Senate from Wisconsin in
1922, was defeated by Robert M. La Follette. But "I had good-
sized audiences and fine enthusiasm wherever I went through the
state," she said, "and I believe my time and money were well spent
in demonstrating the kind of campaign that women can carry on;
that it is possible to go anywhere, come in contact with every kind
of people, go through a strenuous campaign and come out with
one's own self-respect and respect of the people. I feel confident
that the work I have done this fall has blazed the trail for the
women who will seek office in future campaigns."[61]

The assumption that women candidates and officeholders were
primarily wives and mothers remained intact during this period,
and has of course persisted to the present day. A 1929 article
entitled "Women in Public Life," written by a woman lawyer and
Justice Department attorney, enthusiastically enumerated and described women holding offices at various levels. Nonetheless her
concluding argument was that the number of women legislators
should and would increase because of the possibility of combining
public and private roles. "Outside interests are always subservient
to the home; husbands and children have first call on time and

59. *New York Times*, 15 April 1928.
60. *New York Times*, 20 January 1929.
61. *Woman Citizen*, 2 December 1922, 12.

affection. Legislative duties, however, call for attendance only when the legislatures are in session, and the holding of such office enables woman to have a career without sacrifice of home."[62]

Thus one boundary distinguishing political men from political women had to do with women's primary responsibility for family and children and women's presumed lack of ambition. This boundary was not widely contested, and, as we have seen, many women who were in politics took pains to point out that political women were different from political men on these dimensions.

In addition, women were assumed to have, and many publicly claimed, particular interests in social welfare, education, hygiene, and other "women's and children's" issues, as well as issues involving moral conduct. The surge in women's involvement in the presidential campaign of 1928 was widely attributed to the fact that the campaign issues (particularly prohibition and religious tolerance) were the kinds of human and moral questions on which women felt particularly competent to make a judgment.[63]

The women who occupied local offices, especially, were seen as engaging in "municipal housekeeping." Sometimes this involved physical clean-ups, as in Jackson, Wyoming, where the women mayor and city council members installed a system of pipes to replace the open ditch that had previously transported the town's water supply. These Wyoming women and the city council in Thayer, Kansas also counted the establishment of city parks among their accomplishments. Other officeholders focused on "moral house-cleaning," such as "the enforcement of prohibition and the licensing of soft drink parlors," the prevention of bootlegging, "the conviction of gamblers and the inspection of dance halls." One woman "insisted that pool places be closed or minors excluded from them, and that the curfew ordinance be enforced." Mildred Adams, writing in *The American City* in 1922, argued that men and women see the same problems or issues from very different perspectives: "Men think of roads and water and buildings and budgets in terms of engineering. Women translate them into terms of municipal housekeeping. A good housekeeper has well-built, orderly paths; her water-supply is clean, adequate, and conve-

62. Moncure, "Women in Political Life," 643.
63. See, for example, *New York Times Magazine*, 12 August 1928, 1.

niently piped; her house is well made, comfortable, and well kept; she spends and saves on a budget. She goes a step farther—and here is where housekeeping is broader than engineering. She is deeply interested in educating children. She knows how vitally important it is to have them surrounded with the right kind of environment. Therefore, she translates those abstractions into concrete terms, and enters the realm of moral housekeeping."[64]

Though many women officeholders did exhibit a particular interest in women's issues, often pushing to equalize inheritance and other laws and promoting protective and regulatory legislation, contemporary accounts include a number of women whose legislative specialties derived from the particular needs of their constituencies. One article mentions a California legislator serving on the Agricultural, Mines and Mining, and Irrigation Committees to represent the interests of her constituents, as well as a New Mexico woman who "attributes her election to her familiarity with irrigation and drainage problems."

Moreover, conflict sometimes arose when women's issues were *not* the primary focus for individual officeholders. When Mary E. W. Risteau was elected to the Maryland House of Delegates, her goal was to serve on the Agriculture Committee, "the one committee in which Risteau was vitally interested." When the Speaker failed to appoint her to this committee, she issued a public challenge to a fellow farmer serving in the Senate: "I always wanted to get on this committee, and it was quite a shock for a farmer to be left off. I am a better farmer than Magnus Johnson. . . . I can beat him walking behind a plow or driving a tractor." She suggested a contest; meanwhile, the Speaker added her to the Agriculture Committee following a party conference.[65]

A similar account involves a Minnesota legislator, Mrs. Hannah Kempfer. Mrs. Kempfer, a farmer, was mentioned as a potential chairman of the legislature's Conservation, Game and Fish Committee and "her male colleagues did not give it serious consideration"; an observer explained that "man has always assumed that the privilege of hunting and fishing is his; to the women belongs the honor of cooking the food when it is captured." However, Mrs.

64. Adams, "What Women Mayors Are Doing."
65. *New York Times*, 10 January 1924.

Kempfer secured the backing of influential individuals and of the Izaak Walton League and was appointed chairman of the committee. Her colleague from Minneapolis, Mrs. Mabeth Hurd Page, chaired a committee perhaps assumed to be more in line with women's traditional interests, the Public Welfare and Social Legislation Committee.[66]

Nichols describes the women who served in the Connecticut Assembly during the 1920s (forty-seven had been elected by 1931) as being "vocal on women's issues" such as prison conditions, the establishment of a state child welfare bureau, legislation protecting women and child workers, and the appointment of more women factory inspectors.[67] An unsuccessful Democratic House candidate from Pennsylvania campaigned on the slogans "House Cleaning—No Graft—Genuine Prosperity" and "women are good at housecleaning."[68] In New York, women legislators during the twenties included a physician who focused on public health issues and legislation regulating drugs, a teacher who sponsored legislation to finance school building programs and create teaching scholarships, a lawyer who worked to abolish the death penalty and protect children, a prominent suffrage and prohibition leader, and a civic activist who promoted fair rent legislation, increasing teachers' salaries, and increasing the minimum wage.[69]

WHO WERE THE CANDIDATES?

What led women to run for office? Some women had been involved in electoral politics before 1920, as campaign workers and party loyalists. This was particularly true in suffrage states, but a few women were active in the parties even before they had the right to vote, as I discussed in chapter 4. Male party leaders trying to appeal to women voters wanted to list women candidates on their tickets, and the League of Women Voters encouraged its members to get involved in partisan and electoral politics. Not surprisingly, many of the women who ran for office in the early part of the

66. Moncure, "Women in Political Life," 642.
67. Nichols, *Votes and More for Women*, 48–50.
68. *Woman Citizen*, 21 October 1922.
69. Weinstein, *Biographical Sketches of the Women of the New York State Legislature*.

decade, pushed by the League and pulled by the parties, had been active in the suffrage movement; this was true of about half the women who served in state legislatures in the 1920s.[70]

Many, if not most, of the women in electoral politics at the state and national levels came out of, and maintained connections with, women's and social reform organizations. Studies of women's involvement in state politics in this period amply document this connection.[71] "In many states as suffrage opened doors for women in government, male politicians turned to clubs and associations in search of qualified appointees."[72] For example, women who had worked for welfare reform were appointed county welfare directors or to state boards on charities, reformatories, or other institutions. Women pushing for particular legislation (like Albion Fellows Bacon in Indiana, who lobbied for housing reform and other progressive measures), or running for office (like Ruth Hanna McCormick) used their networks of women's club connections to mobilize support. Women who ran for and served in the New York legislature during the twenties and thirties had generally gotten their start in the social reform movement of earlier years, primarily as volunteers. After the passage of the Nineteenth Amendment, reform-oriented organizations such as the New York Women's City Club and the League of Women Voters provided a forum where women could learn political skills.[73]

Grace Abbott, a key member of the women's welfare and reform community during this period, provides an illustration of the connections between electoral politics and the "female dominion" that Muncy describes. Abbott had been the head of the Child Labor Division of the Children's Bureau, which was created to administer the federal child labor law. When the Supreme Court declared this law unconstitutional, the division was disbanded, and after a stint as director of the Illinois State Immigrants' Commission, Abbott decided to return to Nebraska to run for Congress. She was

70. Breckinridge, *Women in the Twentieth Century*, 326–327.

71. See Gordon, *After Winning*; Nichols, *Votes and More for Women*; Jensen, "Disfranchisement is a Disgrace"; Thomas, *The New Woman in Alabama*; and see my analysis in chapter 6.

72. Scott, *Natural Allies*, 157.

73. *Ibid.*; see also Miller, *Ruth Hanna McCormick*; Weinstein, *Biographical Sketches of the Women of the New York State Legislature*, 4.

talked out of this by Julia Lathrop and Florence Kelley, and was then appointed to head the Children's Bureau.

It is worth noting that while candidates were likely to have a background as activists in women's organizations, they held widely differing views on how women's organizations and women voters had contributed to their campaigns. One candidate, from Kansas, said that "women generally supported me, regardless of party," while a California woman said that organized women did very little to assist in her campaign: "the reason, I think, being that 'women in politics' has not yet been accepted as altogether 'proper' and women lack the courage which could make them a mighty power in politics—if they could persuade themselves to get in the game."[74]

As is the case today, women who ran for office in the 1920s tended to be well-educated and middle-class, and to have either a professional background, experience in voluntary organizations, or both. Breckinridge conducted a survey of women who had been state legislators in the 1920s. She received responses from 126 of the 320 who had served. Of these, 26 had been teachers, 9 lawyers, 2 doctors, 6 businesswomen, and 3 social workers. Twenty-six had held office before. A few said they had been against woman suffrage; about half had been active in the suffrage movement. Moncure's study in 1929, describing women state legislators, estimated that "approximately 33 percent are housewives in addition to their lawmaking activities, 18 percent are teachers, only 10 percent are business women and 8 percent are writers and lecturers. Among the remainder we find social service workers, farmers, lawyers, nurses and doctors. Strange to say, only 3 percent of these lawmakers are lawyers, although many are the daughters or wives of lawyers. The educational qualifications of women are probably higher than those of their male colleagues, as approximately 84 percent have had college or university training."[75] In 1928, a journalist observed that while there were a variety of types of women in politics, "the women who have attained high party office vary within surprisingly narrow limits. A composite feminine Who's Who in national party councils in the current campaign would disclose a woman of 50, who looks 40—who is smartly dressed, who is

74. *Woman Citizen*, 2 December 1922, 11.

75. Breckinridge, *Women in the Twentieth Century;* Moncure, "Women in Political Life."

financially comfortable, and who possesses social charm. Her children are grown. . . . More often than not she has already had some sort of commercial, professional or volunteer organizing experience."[76]

Though it would be difficult to describe a typical woman candidate of the 1920s, an account of the career of Alice Lorraine Daly, who ran unsuccessfully for governor of South Dakota in 1922, illustrates some of the themes and connections common to many of the women active in electoral politics during this period. Educated in Boston, Daly came to South Dakota to head the Department of Public Speaking at the State Normal School. She became involved in the Woman's Peace Party and the League of Women Voters. In 1920 the Nonpartisan League party nominated her for state superintendent of public instruction, in 1922 for governor. In recounting the experiences and images which had impelled her into public life, she described "the cry of undernourished children echoing through unkempt day coaches, as they lumbered over South Dakota prairies; . . . the dearth of good homes among our workers; the lack of educational opportunities for our rural children. . . ." Campaigning in part "against the weaknesses of our present outworn economic system, and for a more modern system of finance, credit, public control and ownership," Daly argued that women "believe more than men that economic conditions may be controlled, which is one of the reasons why she thinks it is a good idea to have a women for governor. It is, she says, a state housekeeping job."[77] Daly's background—well-educated and active in women's organizations—probably characterized the majority of women candidates for political office in the twenties. She espoused what were thought to be women's issues—concern for opportunities and protection for women and children and a focus on social justice. Like the women in rural New York whom Paula Baker studied, Daly and many women like her were comfortable with the idea of government intervention, and like many women candidates she extended the housekeeping metaphor to include the office she was seeking.

76. Barnard, "Women Who Wield Political Power," 6.
77. *Woman Citizen*, 7 October 1922.

Once nationwide suffrage for women was a reality, the idea that women could and should run for political office, though not much talked about during the suffrage campaign, seemed obvious to many women. Beyond the few token women congressional candidates and governors, the decade of the twenties saw a steadily growing number of women serving in state legislatures and in county, city and town offices. I argued in chapter 2 that women's citizenship in the U.S. had long been seen as indirect, exercised primarily through a woman's care of husband and children, and disinterested, rather than self-interested. Over the decade of the 1920s, women occupying elected political office, formerly a rare spectacle indeed, became relatively common, as we have seen. However, the persisting assumptions that women politicians' primary responsibility was their family, that their policy concerns stemmed from their domestic responsibilities, and that they were not politically ambitious carried these distinct images of women's citizenship along as women entered public life. Women were assumed to be political beings of a different kind than men—to retain their womanly nature, they needed to downplay personal ambition, accentuate women's issues and goals, and remember that their families came first. But even the women candidates and oficeholders who, while eschewing political ambition and putting their families first, still campaigned, gave speeches, bargained and argued, helped to transform the relationship between gender and public leadership. And, as indicated by the stories of Mabel Walker Willebrandt and the women legislators who expressed interests in farming or engineering, such boundaries were permeable. A few women in the twenties saw themselves as politicians not too different from their male counterparts. Ruth Hanna McCormick, who was "first, last, and always a politician" and unafraid to categorize herself as such, in this context foreshadows the seventies more than she typifies the twenties. The gender differences that grounded the newly constituted boundaries for women candidates and officeholders in the twenties were generally agreed to be "natural" and thus accepted by both men and women.

"Don't Order Them by Basket"
(Cartoon by Carey Orr. © Copyrighted Chicago Tribune
Company, photograph courtesy the Carey Orr Collection,
Syracuse University Library.)

S I X   Women and Electoral
          Politics after Suffrage

I think we might legitimately ask whether as a democracy we
have gone forward in the past twenty-one years, and take it
for granted that if we have, it means that the majority of the
women, as well as the majority of the men, have justified their
right to suffrage.

Eleanor Roosevelt, writing in *Good Housekeeping* in 1940

When I was growing up in Omaha in the 1950s, both my parents, but especially my father, along with many of his friends and associates, were active in the Republican party. I loved election campaigns: we children got to put signs up in our yard, help hand out campaign literature, and listen to speeches. I particularly liked election day itself, when my father, who was designated by the party organization as a "flying judge," would travel from polling place to polling place checking on the progress of the voting. This allowed me into places I'd otherwise never see, like firehouses in the Stockyards district of South Omaha, where convivial Republican and Democratic officials sat drinking coffee and eating sausage sandwiches, and the experience gave me a lifelong sense of the enjoyable rituals associated with elections and voting. Looking back at this experience now, I see that my ideas about the kinds of people who were partisan activists (though not candidates or officeholders) were quite gender-neutral: both women and men handed out literature, stuffed envelopes, served as election judges and poll watchers and drank coffee and ate sandwiches. These images were formed only a little more than thirty years after the Nineteenth Amendment was passed, only a little more than thirty years after ballots were no longer cast in barbershops and saloons. American political culture changed during this period, moving even further away from the intensely male political rituals and "allowing women in," at least to the extent that a nine-year-old might perceive women in flowered dresses and hats to be doing politics right along with the men. But if I had looked beyond the firehouse, at the county courthouse or the state legislature, or for that matter at the places where important decisions were made about party matters, I would have seen mostly men. And if I had talked with the women party members, I probably would have discovered that they still perceived clear boundaries delineating appropriate behavior and political work for men and for women.

In many ways, the boundaries negotiated for women in partisan and electoral politics in the 1920s remained in place until they were directly challenged by women beginning in the 1970s. Electoral politics was changed only slightly by the entry of women— women may have been changed more—but by their very presence, as well as the distinct interests and political style they brought to politics, women entering politics in the 1920s began to change the way Americans thought about politics and politicians. The position that "nothing really happened" with the passage of the Nineteenth Amendment has always seemed shortsighted to me. The previous chapters have documented the measurable changes that took place over the decade—the increase in women's registration and voting, the changes in party rules to adapt to suffrage, the opening up of some government positions to women. At the same time it is clear that the boundary which had been drawn to exclude women from electoral politics was not erased but was renegotiated, so that women, for the most part, had a special and relatively powerless place in American party and electoral politics by the end of the 1920s. What implications did this new boundary have for American politics? In what ways did woman suffrage make a difference in the ways politics was carried on?

CHANGING THE FACE OF POLITICS

In the late nineteenth century, political campaigns—the heart of what Americans considered politics—consisted of "spectacular displays of exuberant partisanship. Through participation in torchlight

parades, mass rallies, and campaign clubs and marching companies, men gave expression to [their] partisan outlook . . ."[1] Well
before 1920, however, changes in the press, in the regulation and
state control of parties and voting, and in communications technol-
ogy had transformed campaigns of mobilization into campaigns of
education and advertising.[2] Nonetheless, as the suffrage debates
in state after state made clear, politics and partisanship continued
to be associated with manhood and male virtues well into the twentieth century.

Woman suffrage did much to erode this connection. Perhaps
the easiest changes to document have to do with the impact that
voting women had on the voting itself: on the places people voted,
their behavior while voting, and perhaps on the meanings they
attached to voting. In October 1920 a *New York Times* writer observed the registration at city polling places: "Where is all the
election-time atmosphere of yesteryear? Where are the . . . polling
places blue with smoke? 'It ain't like it used to be,' intoned the
veteran policeman on guard during the recent registration. . . .
'And no trouble, never no trouble any more,' [he] regretted. 'In
the old days we could always run in a couple of guys, there was
always rows. There's nothing doing any more. Since the women's
been mixing in, politics ain't the same.' "[3]

Balloting had often taken place in clearly male domains such as
barbershops, saloons, or pool halls. This had to change once
women comprised, at least potentially, a large portion of the electorate, so that schools, churches, firehouses, and other gender-
neutral public places were pushed into service as polling places.
This gave elections a more "sober" air, thought the *Woman Citizen,* which commented on the "increased use of school-houses for
polling places. An election in a public-school building gives to
voting the character of a dignified civic institution. In New York
City the use of schools and churches has grown rapidly since the
enfranchisement of women." Simply the presence of women added

1. McGerr, "Political Style and Women's Power," 23.

2. McGerr, "Political Style and Women's Power"; Richard Jensen, *The Winning
of the Midwest* (Chicago: University of Chicago Press, 1971).

3. *New York Times,* 17 October 1920, sec. 8, p. 1.

a note of dignity and from many sources came reports of increased courtesy at the polls. The *Woman Citizen* noted a lessening of "rowdyism" at voting places and remarked on the courtesy of party officials and attending policemen. Not only were many voters now women, but most polling places, beginning in 1921 or 1922 if not in 1920, saw the presence of women election officials and poll watchers. The *Woman Citizen,* in an article in 1922, quoted from the *Cincinnati Inquirer:* "the election was marked by fewer disputes at the polls than any in the memory of the oldest member of the Board of Elections."[4]

Through the twenties and beyond, party organizations, even if they were not willing to give real power to women activists, were quite willing to have women share the burden of canvassing, staffing party headquarters, and serving as poll watchers and election clerks. The *Woman Citizen* commented on the general improvement of the quality of election officials since suffrage, reminding readers that one of the arguments against suffrage was that elections had been held in disreputable places and supervised by disreputable men and "that ladies would be contaminated by contact with them. The argument seemed to be based on the supposition that dirt and ignorance and even violence were necessary concomitants of elections."[5] It seems fair to say that woman suffrage hastened the decline of the view of elections as somewhat questionable, probably corrupt activities and encouraged the view of elections as a wholesome community event in which all good citizens could participate.[6]

At higher levels, too, there were inroads made into the relentlessly male world of party and electoral politics. Observers of the party conventions in the 1920s routinely commented on the changes attributed to women's participation: less smoking, less pro-

4. *Woman Citizen,* 18 November 1921; 8 November 1922; *New York Times,* 10 October 1920, 5.

5. *Woman Citizen,* 5 November 192, 12.

6. John Reynolds' study of New Jersey carefully documents the changes in voting behavior and party organizations that resulted from the institution of Progressive reforms. He concludes that "Community-based partisan activity that had made voting an open and social act gave way to a more bureaucratic and private function supervised by the state. Because voting was no longer a social function the cult of good citizenship would also admit women." Reynolds, *Testing Democracy,* 172.

fanity, more dignified proceedings. Certainly the practice of sub-mitting questionnaires to candidates and bringing candidates to-gether to speak from the same platform, which the League of Women Voters began in the 1920s, altered the way campaigns were conducted.[7] In 1920, Anne O'Hagan Shinn, writing in the *New York Times*, noted that women had even changed (to some extent) how and where politics was practiced. Remarking on the commit-ment and seriousness of the women delegates, alternates, and other participants, she said they had "caused sacred precedents to be smashed. . . . They had made 9 a.m. instead of 3 a.m.—or perhaps, more exactly, as well as 3 a.m.—a popular hour for the consideration of political problems, and melon and toast instead of merely tobacco the accompaniment of political discussion."[8] By 1928, the *New York Times* found a burgeoning number of women campaign workers, and claimed that "if anything, women outnum-ber men at political meetings, and women speakers are becoming as numerous as men."[9] A wonderful illustration of women's at-tempt to change some of the material symbols of politics is an anecdote concerning one of the first two women elected to the New York State Assembly in 1918, Ida Sammis. According to politi-cal legend, "Sammis' first unofficial act was to take her brass spit-toon—each member of the Assembly was allocated one—and pol-ish it to a brilliant shine. She filled it with flowers and placed it on her desk. . . ."[10]

In these ways the face of party and electoral politics changed during the 1920s. It ceased to be unimaginable that women would speak at national conventions, attend party meetings, or run for office. But women with positions of real power in the partisan and electoral arenas were still rare—and continued to be rare for at

7. *New York Times*, 30 April 1928, 20. Some resistance to these new practices emerged. In Delaware, when the League of Women Voters asked legislators whether they supported various League positions, the legislature responded by passing a law making it illegal to "intimidate" candidates and legislators with ques-tionnaires. Young, *In the Public Interest*, 56.

8. *New York Times*, 5 July 1920, sec. 7, p. 1.

9. McCormick, "Enter Women, the New Boss of Politics."

10. Helene E. Weinstein, *Lawmakers: Biographical Sketches of the Women of the New York State Legislature (1918–1988)* (Albany: New York State Library, 1989), 4.

least fifty more years. "In the absence of female politicians as role models," write Linda Witt et al. in 1994, "women previously had to imagine themselves as politicians, the most male of roles. . . . A 1974 study of women who were deeply involved in local party politics, a likely source of prospective candidates, found most of them could not see themselves in office. Two thirds of those surveyed thought running would not be 'proper.'"[11]

Nonetheless the boundary had been changed, and just as women were increasingly moving into new occupations and professions in the 1920s, positions for women in government and politics opened up after suffrage. Breckinridge enumerated the women who held significant Presidential appointments in the Federal government: there were fifteen in 1930, compared with five in 1920. She also commented on the increased numbers of women appointed to special federal commissions and committees. Lemons documented many other federal appointees, arguing that in the 1920s "women entered nearly every aspect of the government." In 1919, women constituted just over 10% of the country's postmasters (these appointments were partly political—though Civil Service examinations were given, any of the top three candidates could be appointed). By 1930 women comprised almost 18% of the postmasters, their numbers having increased over the decade from 255 to 940. There was even greater growth in the number of women in local elective and appointive offices; as Breckinridge pointed out, "while modest progress in conspicuous federal or state offices has been hailed with joy and desired with fervor, the substantial advance in local office holding has been almost entirely ignored."[12] A series of articles in *Public Personnel Studies* in 1930 described the variety of local, national and international positions held by women.[13]

11. Linda Witt, Karen M. Paget and Glenna Matthews, *Running as a Woman: Gender and Power in American Politics* (New York: Free Press, 1994), citing Marcia M. Lee, "Why Few Women Hold Public Office," in *Portrait of Marginality*, ed. Marianne Githens and Jewell Prestage (New York: Longman, 1977).

12. Breckinridge, *Women in the Twentieth Century*, ch. 18, and see ch. 5; Lemons, *The Woman Citizen*, 77.

13. Avis Marion Saint, "Women in the Public Service: General Survey" *Public Personnel Studies* 8:4 (1930), 46–54; "Women in the Public Service: The City of Berkeley," *Public Personnel Studies* 8:7 (1930), 104–7; "Women in the Public Service: The City of Oakland," *Public Personnel Studies* 8:8 (1930), 119–22.

The process of redefining the boundary that distinguished between appropriate male and female behavior in public life threw into some question the traditional relationship between gender and citizenship. That is, as women voted in growing numbers, as they ran for public office, and as they were appointed to public office, sustaining the idea that their political participation was somehow completely different from men's—less direct and more disinterested—became increasingly untenable. Many political women themselves, of course, continued to insist on women's unique political stance. As Witt, Paget and Matthews have argued, "the tradition of altruism might prepare a woman politician to play up her gender, but it prepared very few to be partisan politicians, let alone to run for office."[14] But just as the presence of women at the polls changed Americans' image of the voter, women working in partisan and electoral politics in the 1920s were laying the groundwork for women like Eleanor Roosevelt, Molly Dewson, Frances Perkins, and Helen Gahagan Douglas, who balanced their disinterestedness with a tougher and more pragmatic outlook.

CHANGING POLITICAL PRACTICE

During the long period when women were excluded from electoral politics, they developed an alternative set of political forms and organizational strategies to accomplish their goals. Nancy Cott has claimed that "women's organizations pioneered in, accepted, and polished modern methods of pressure-group politics."[15] This includes lobbying and coalition-building, both of which were much more commonly engaged in by women's organizations than by men's organizations during the Progressive era and into the 1920s. Especially before 1920, women were forced to enter into coalitions with other groups such as labor unions and male reform groups. In her case study of the formation of the Cook County Juvenile Court, Victoria Getis shows how members of the Chicago Women's Club, who began working on the issue of the state's treatment of children in the 1890s, formed coalitions with the Illinois State Conference of Charities and Corrections and the Chicago Bar As-

14. Witt, Paget and Matthews, *Running as a Woman*, 33–34.
15. Cott, *The Grounding of Modern Feminism*, 97.

sociation in order to get the relevant state legislation passed.[16] Breckinridge wrote in 1933 that

> women began their work as lobbyists long before they were granted the vote. Anti-slavery agitation, suffrage, temperance, less cruel treatment of the insane, international agreements for mitigating the horrors of war, were causes to which women devoted their efforts, seeking definite and important community gains without the power of the ballot. What could not be done directly had to be done indirectly. Women had neither funds nor political backing but they had a great belief that legislators who understood would eventually respond to the facts which they presented and the conclusions to be drawn from those facts. In 1900, for example, the General Federation of Women's Clubs resolved 'to work for legislation for women and children so that the law of every state will equal the best already enacted,' and the technique of this work with legislatures was elaborately described. Speeches on methods of lobbying occupied a place on the programs of meetings and in 1914 and 1916 conferences were held at which the successful methods were discussed.[17]

A recent analysis by sociologist Elisabeth Clemens explains convincingly both why these kinds of political tactics were adopted by women's organizations and how such innovations influenced the behavior of other groups. Clemens argues that the introduction and effective use of such alternative models of organizational work had the effect, in specific instances, of producing countering changes in the strategies of other groups (one example is the California Womens Christian Temperance Union and the opposing liquor interests). In general, she argues against Robert Michels's

16. Victoria Getis, "Doing the Work of Government: the Chicago Woman's Club and Progressive Reform" (paper presented at the meetings of the Social Science History Association, Baltimore, MD, November 1993).

17. Sophonisba P. Breckinridge, "The Activities of Women Outside the Home," 739.

conception of conservative, unilinear organizational change and for a more context-sensitive model which recognizes that "the very process of challenging political institutions can change the rules of political action, if not necessarily the substance of political outcomes."[18]

Women's groups adapted existing models of nonpolitical organization for political purposes. For example, mobilizing directly as a voting bloc was obviously not a feasible strategy prior to suffrage, and thus women's groups were not faced with the necessity of securing the membership's unanimous or majority agreement with particular organizational goals. Consequently the groups tended to have departmental or federated structures, allowing small groups or local organizations to focus on a range of different goals. Even the Women's Joint Congressional Committee, formed in 1920 to centralize the lobbying efforts of women's groups, took no positions itself but rather facilitated the work of sub-groups of three or more organizations which took the same stand on an issue.[19] During the 1920s, women's associations used a variety of strategies (as they had before, in the "Front Door Lobby" which prodded congressmen to support suffrage). These included maintaining card indexes on "every important officeholder in Washington," publishing research, visiting members of Congress and federal officials, forming grass roots delegations, keeping "close contact with the Women's and Children's Bureaus," and working with key women in the Republican and Democratic parties.[20] Lobbying was not new, but in the nineteenth century it had been associated with corrupt practices and often aimed to produce private bills. When women's organizations adapted lobbying practices, what was new were their efforts to educate leaders and to move public opinion on specific issues through the use of expert testimony, public education campaigns, and grass-roots pressure. By combining the "tainted model" of the

18. Clemens, "Organizational Repertoires and Institutional Change," 793.

19. Clemens, "Organizational Repertoires and Institutional Change," 758, 766–67; also see Dorothy Johnson, "Organized Women Lobbyists in the 1920s," *Capitol Studies* 1 (1972), 43.

20. Johnson, "Organized Women Lobbyists in the 1920s," 44; for a description of the "Front Door Lobby," see Maud Wood Park, *Front Door Lobby* (Boston: Beacon Press, 1960).

lobby with the educational strategies common to nineteenth-century women's organizations, lobbying was transformed and legitimated as an accepted form of political action. But as Clemens points out, "the politics of education and public opinion ran into difficulty when women attempted to translate research and expertise into political influence"; the merging of educational and legislative strategies proved difficult.[21]

Here the changing face of electoral politics in the 1920s and the entry of more women into partisan activism helped solidify the new political form of lobbying. Whereas before suffrage those who would propose, consider, vote on, and implement any given measure were all men, now a few women sympathetic to the agenda of women's groups occupied positions in legislatures and agencies. When Julia Lathrop, head of the Children's Bureau, wanted to increase congressional appropriations for the Bureau in 1912, she "mobilized club women and reformers to lobby their congressmen and convinced newspapers and magazines such as the *Ladies' Home Journal* to write favorable articles about the Bureau's work."[22] In 1921, when she supported Grace Abbott's appointment as her successor, she could use similar techniques but could now also call upon women on the Republican National Committee to exert their influence.[23]

The opening up of politics to women in the 1920s created a new situation for women reformers such as Grace and Edith Abbott, Sophonisba Breckinridge, Florence Kelley, Katherine Bement Davis and many others at the state and local levels. These women often went back and forth between administrative positions in the charitable sector and more strictly political positions—for example, Katherine Bement Davis, who had a Ph.D. in political economy from the University of Chicago, was appointed superintendent of the Bedford Hills, New York Reformatory for Women but later

21. Clemens, Organizational Repertoires and Institutional Change, 774–75, 783–84.

22. Molly Ladd-Taylor, "Hull House Goes to Washington: Women and the Childrens Bureau," in *Gender, Class, Race, and Reform in the Progressive Era*, ed. Noralee Frankel and Nancy S. Dye (Lexington: University Press of Kentucky, 1991), 113.

23. Muncy, *Creating a Female Dominion*, 33, 88.

was asked by the mayor of New York City to serve as his Commissioner of Corrections. In both these positions, Davis was politically active, supporting Roosevelt in 1912 and Republican candidates at other times. She drew on her political experience and skills when she lobbied the New York Legislature for prison reform legislation.[24] And even those women reformers who never were involved wholeheartedly in major party politics were politically skilled and influential. Grace Abbott, Sophonisba Breckinridge, and Julia Lathrop were not only professional social scientists but were highly skilled politicians and lobbyists as well, campaigning during the 1920s for the Shepard- Towner legislation, the child labor amendment, and other reform measures; in the 1930s they were friendly critics of Roosevelt's policies.[25]

Moreover, there were extensive connections between women who were party leaders and the members of the "female dominion." Grace Abbott deliberated in 1921 about running for public office in Nebraska, her home state, rather than succeeding Julia Lathrop as Chief of the Children's Bureau in the Department of Labor. Her appointment was backed by Harriet Taylor Upton and Katherine Phillips Edson, both members of the Republican National Committee.[26] Later, during FDR's administration, Abbott could not publicly support the appointment of Frances Perkins to head the Labor Department, but she could put to work her political expertise and connections: "she understood the use of influence in Washington and had other means [than public statements] at hand. In December [1932] she arranged a conference on the problems of children in the Depression and invited Perkins to be the principal speaker. When Perkins arrived in Washington, she was astonished to find that Abbott had also arranged for her to be photographed, interviewed, and introduced to Senators and congressmen on Capitol Hill."[27]

When Ruth McCormick ran for office, she depended heavily on

24. Fitzpatrick, *Endless Crusade*, ch. 5.

25. Fitzpatrick, *Endless Crusade*; Costin, *Two Sisters for Social Justice*; Muncy, *Creating a Female Dominion*.

26. Costin, *Two Sisters for Social Justice*, 121–122.

27. Costin, *Two Sisters for Social Justice*, 213.

a network of politically active women, both those with whom she had worked for suffrage and members of various Chicago reform groups. "Without their support she would not have had the strength she needed to meet men on equal terms, the secret of her success in the 1920s."[28] Similarly, Sandra Schackel describes how the "political skills and expertise" that women learned in helping to reform New Mexico's social welfare system in the 1920s "laid the groundwork for continued political power in later decades."[29] Mabel Walker Willebrandt, when she was pushing for prison reform from her political appointment as assistant attorney general (specifically, she was trying to establish the first federal prison for women), called on the Women's Joint Congressional Committee, Republican party leader Harriet Taylor Upton, the General Federation of Women's Clubs, and the Women Lawyers Association.[30]

Those women who did run for and attain elective office frequently had backgrounds in social work or education.[31] Ellen Sullivan Woodward from Mississippi, who had served in the Mississippi House of Representatives in the mid-1920s, was the state's Democratic national committeewoman for many years, and had long experience in the Mississippi Federation of Women's Clubs, was named Director of Women's Relief Programs of the Federal Emergency Relief Administration in 1933, and later became director of its successor, the Works Progress Administration. Other southern Democratic party activists received appointments during the New

28. Miller, *Ruth Hanna McCormick,* 99.

29. Sandra Schackel, *Social Housekeepers: Women Shaping Public Policy in New Mexico, 1920–1940* (Albuquerque: University of New Mexico Press, 1992), 169.

30. Dorothy M. Brown, "Power in Washington: Networking in the 1920s from Willebrandt to Roosevelt." Paper presented at the Conference on Women, Politics and Change, New School for Social Research (1990).

31. In fact this continues to be true today. For example, of the 65 women who served in Congress between 1920 and 1968, almost 60% of those who listed a previous occupation (42% of all 65) were in education, social work, or government (Gruberg, *Women in American Politics,* 120). Over half the women state legislators studied by the Center for the American Woman and Politics in 1988, over half had "traditionally female" former occupations such as social worker, nurse, librarian or teacher. See Debra Dodson and Susan Carroll, *Reshaping the Agenda: Women in State Legislatures* (New Brunswick: Center for the American Woman and Politics, Rutgers University, 1991), 109, 114.

Deal, including Johnetta Spelman and Pattie Jacobs.[32] Adelina Otero-Warren, who was active in the Republican party in New Mexico and ran for Congress in 1922, had served on the state's first Board of Public Health and as Santa Fe County's superintendent of schools.[33] Of the twenty-eight women in Susan Ware's collective biography, *Beyond Suffrage: Women in the New Deal*, fourteen had done substantial work in the parties (e.g., as committeewomen or Democratic National Committee staff) and/or in elective office (as governors, members of Congress, or state legislators).

The connections between women's groups, women in federal and state agencies, and women party leaders and officeholders made the integration of educational and legislative strategies that much easier in the 1920s and the 1930s. Policy analysts might call these links "issue networks" today, and indeed their existence and effectiveness, I suggest, contributed to the decline of party politics and the rise of interest group politics.

CHANGING THE POLITICAL CALCULUS

As I argued in chapter 1, judgments about the success or impact of woman suffrage have been based on expectations of substantial changes in political outcomes. When such changes did not materialize, contemporary as well as more recent analysts judged woman suffrage to be politically ineffective. But instead of asking, "did women's vote accomplish what some suffragists claimed it would?" what if we were to base our judgments on the question, "what changes took place that would not have occurred without women as voters?"

First of all, we could certainly argue that women extended the life of Progressivism. Shackel's recent study of New Mexico women concludes that "In matters of health, education, labor, and social justice, women kept the reform impulse alive between World War I and the New Deal. . . . At the national level, women lobbied determinedly for a child labor law, mother's pensions, and social security. In their local communities, women raised funds for parks

32. Martha H. Swain, "The Public Role of Southern Women," in *Sex, Race, and the Role of Women in the South*, ed. Joanne V. Hawks and Sheila Skemp (Jackson: University Press of Mississippi (1983), 39.

33. Schackel, *Social Housekeepers*, 33, 46.

and playgrounds, petitioned for sewage systems, looked after needy families and helped establish institutions for the blind, deaf, and delinquent."[34] In other words, "newly enfranchised women carried elements of [Progressivism] right into the otherwise reactionary 1920s."[35] This last phrase is significant: the success or failure of women's agenda must be placed in the political context of the increasing conservatism and red-baiting that characterized the 1920s. As Carole Nichols says, "The Connecticut experience suggests that even a highly organized and unified feminist movement would not have effected political or social change in the state in the 1920s. The major responsibility for the failure of reform efforts in Connecticut lay with the male politicians and their business and farmer allies."[36]

Nonetheless, both at the national and state levels, more was accomplished by reform-minded women in the 1920s than is sometimes recognized. Their successes did not end with the Cable Act and the Shepard-Towner Act. Breckinridge describes these two pieces of legislation as women's signal early successes in the 1920s, but goes on to list the Personnel Reclassification Act, legislation regulating interstate and foreign commerce in agricultural products, the creation of a new federal prison for women offenders, and the Child Labor Amendment (passed by Congress but not ratified by the states). In 1930, she concludes, "looking back a decade, a total of 436 state and local laws enacted with the support of [the Women's Joint Congressional Committee] can be listed. There have been 61 dealing with child welfare, 130 removing limitations on the rights of women, 75 on social hygiene, 69 in the field of education, 76 dealing with efficiency in government and several on living costs."[37] The policy accomplishments of women's groups in Alabama, for example (along with many unsuccessful

34. Schackel. *Social Housekeepers,* 167.
35. Scott, *Natural Allies,* 171.
36. Nichols, *Votes and More for Women,* 47.
37. Breckinridge, "The Activities of Women Outside the Home," 740–41. As an example of some of these changes in state laws, in Connecticut, local Leagues of Women Voters had success in cities and towns at enacting charter revisions, conservation policies, school construction, citizenship education, and building recreational facilities (Nichols, *Votes and More for Women,* 3).

reform attempts) were the product of cooperation between the state League of Women Voters and the Alabama Federation of Women's Clubs, which together with several other women's groups created the Legislative Council of Alabama Women in 1921. The work of the Council, in turn, was facilitated by the fact that several of its leaders were active and successful in party politics.[38] Many new women's associations, which arose or expanded to fill the void left by the conclusion of suffrage work and the disappearance of NAWSA, worked hard to promote a variety of Progressive measures in Congress in the 1920s, sometimes via the Women's Joint Congressional Committee and often in coalitions with other groups. The successes of these coalitions included expanded appropriations for the Women's and Children's Bureaus through 1924, the Packers and Stockyards Control Act (1921), establishment of the U.S. Coal Commission (1921), outlawing shipment of "filled milk" (1923), civil service reclassification (1924), compulsory school attendance for the District of Columbia (1925), federal funding for home economics instruction equal to other forms of vocational education (1929), the Hawes Cooper Act to prevent competition of prison-made goods with private industry (1929), defeat of proposals threatening land rights of Indians (1924), and the Federal Water Power Act Amendment of 1922, which prohibited private interests from acquiring water rights in national parks.[39]

Robyn Muncy solidifies and expands the work of other historians in describing the emergence of what she calls a "female dominion in the mostly male empire of policymaking." Starting with the establishment of the federal Children's Bureau in the Department of Labor in 1912, continuing with the establishment of similar departments in many states, strengthened by institutions such as schools of social work, its policies advocated (after 1920) by the Women's Joint Congressional Committee, "this network of organizations, female professionals and their followers preserved for the New Deal the reform values and strategies of the Progressive era."[40]

38. Thomas, *The New Woman in Alabama.*
39. Lemons, *The Woman Citizen,* ch. 2; Johnson, "Organized Women Lobbyists."
40. Muncy, *Creating a Female Dominion,* xii.

It is generally agreed, however, that the political success of the women's groups declined during the latter part of the 1920s. The explanation offered by Lemons and others has been that "Congressmen feared a women's bloc initially; and it appeared to have taken shape in the WJCC. However, as a women's vote failed to materialize, legislators became less amenable. Politicians found that women divided like men." Johnson concurs: "it became clear that women did not vote in as large numbers as men and that there was no solidarity in the way they cast their ballots. Congressmen, therefore, need not fear as much retaliation at the polls if they voted against women's measures as they had originally thought."[41] In addition, the increasingly conservative political atmosphere affected women's organizations both through their membership and through the accusations of red-baiters, who targeted women's groups particularly. Given this political context it is not surprising that the gains made in the latter part of the decade were "fewer and more difficult to achieve," as Lemons says, but I believe it is wrong to assume that congressmen simply returned to voting as if women were not a part of the electorate.

Research in political science has told us a great deal about the way members of Congress and other legislators make decisions. They consider individual issues in the context of their constituency, using their knowledge of the demographics and opinion of the public, their own personal experience, and their understanding of the organized groups that will be likely to take a position on the issue. Assuming that they want to retain their seat, representatives take future elections into account when making decisions: if I vote in this way, how can my (potential) opponents use it against me in the next election?[42] In other words, members of Congress in the 1920s, like representatives today, would have been influenced by party leadership and fellow members when making decisions, but their primary criteria would have revolved around the assumptions they made and the knowledge they could obtain about their constituency.

41. Lemons, *The Woman Citizen*, 57; Johnson, "Organized Women Lobbyists," 54.
42. John Kingdon, *Congressmen's Voting Decisions* (New York: Harper & Row, 1973); Richard Fenno, *Home Style* (Boston: Little Brown, 1978).

How might the changing contours of the electorate in the 1920s have affected the typical congressional decision calculus? Recent research has clearly demonstrated the dangers (for political elites) associated with uncertainty about the preferences of a constituency, and, conversely, the strong drive toward acquiring information to reduce uncertainty.[43] If members of Congress could safely assume that women voted at a uniformly low rate, and that those who voted did so just like their husbands, then their knowledge of their constituencies would not be changed by woman suffrage. This seems highly unlikely, for several reasons. First, as detailed in chapter 3, women voted (or registered) at very different rates depending on the state or county they lived in and probably on their class and ethnicity as well. Parties tried to mobilize women voters when it was useful for them to do so, seeing them in those instances as a potentially useful local bloc. Second, in many places throughout the country, though certainly not in all the cases where they tried, organized women had a clear impact on the outcome of elections. In 1921 the *Woman Citizen* reported on some such instances:

> [Women] are said to have helped the defeat of Senator
> New of Indiana, . . . and in the nomination of Albert
> Beveridge. They claim the credit of being largely respon-
> sible for the defeat of the machine in Pennsylvania and
> the nomination of Gifford Pinchot for governor. They
> were also active in Iowa, where Colonel Brookhart, a
> progressive, if not a radical, was nominated; in North
> Dakota where Senator McCumber lost the nomination
> to Lynn J. Frazier, at one time non-partisan governor;
> and in Nebraska where R. B. Howell won the Republi-
> can nomination for the Senate. Mr. Howell is also a pro-
> gressive and was originally an advocate of both prohibi-
> tion and woman suffrage. . . . They made a determined
> fight against the nomination of Senator Reed of Mis-
> souri, and while they did not succeed in defeating him,
> he had to make the fight of his life . . .[44]

43. For example, Linda L. Fowler and Robert D. McClure, *Political Ambition* (New Haven: Yale University Press, 1989), ch. 3.
44. *Woman Citizen,* 26 August 1922, 21.

There were other elections in which the League of Women Voters or other women's groups acted to defeat candidates of the political machine: examples include the defeat of Theodore Bilbo in Mississippi in 1923 and the re-election of a threatened suffrage supporter in Tennessee.[45] There were spectacular failures, too, like Senator James Wadsworth's landslide re-election in New York in 1920. These efforts to punish suffrage opponents or protect supporters generally took place during the first part of the decade and became progressively more rare. As women were mobilized by or attracted to both parties, it became less likely that women's groups would organize for or against a particular candidate. Nonetheless, women's ability to organize politically under the appropriate circumstances was established in these and many other cases.

Third, there can be little doubt that well into the decade both men and women, elites and citizens, perceived women and men to be quite different politically, and that both men and women believed women to have distinct political preferences. This perception may not always have been accurate (see chapter 3 with regard to the 1928 election on this score) but it was pervasive and consistent. Members of Congress in the 1920s, following decision rules based largely on possible electoral consequences, took women into account in ways they did not need to formerly. This can be seen most easily in situations where organized women, nationally or locally, had taken a position. When the Shepard-Towner legislation was initially passed, "the WJCC organizations provided the heavy and sustained pressure that was necessary to bring the issue to a successful vote. Awareness of their vigilance definitely affected the action of Congressmen."[46]

The lobbying network of the "child welfare dominion" remained intact and powerful even after the demise of the Women's Joint Congressional Committee. When Franklin Roosevelt's Social Security legislation was tied up in the House Ways and Means Committee in 1935, the administration asked Grace Abbott to help garner

45. Lemons, *The Woman Citizen,* 91–103.
46. Johnson, "Organized Women Lobbyists," 47. Eleanor Roosevelt described the change succinctly. "There was a time when no one asked 'what will the women think about this?' Now that question comes up often." Eleanor Roosevelt, "Women in Politics," *Good Housekeeping* 110 (March 1940), 45.

support for the bill in order to get it out of committee. Abbott organized a committee to contact "leaders of public opinion," who in turn presented a statement to Congress urging action on the pending bill. "As always, she pulled into play her vast web of women's organizations, which bombarded Congress with letters and telegrams of support for the social security bill in general and the children's programs in particular. Although congressmen themselves showed the least interest in the sections on children, their staffs received more mail in support of those programs than in support of any other section of the social security."[47] Kathryn Kish Sklar describes the National Consumer's League as exemplifying "the vitality of women's grass-roots organizations" in contrast to the structure of male groups—for example, the American Association for Labor Legislation, which took similar stands to the NCL but "preferred to remain an elite group of experts without local affiliates."[48]

Thus, while the measurable impact of women's vote may have declined during the 1920s (as indicated by fewer progressive positions taken or fewer legislative successes), electoral and legislative politics had changed irreversibly. As Lemons says, "The tiger may have swallowed the lady, but he was never quite the same again."[49] As voters, partisans, and officeholders, women were no longer without political resources and now had to be taken into account somehow. Aside from the accounts of the successes and failures of women's lobbying efforts, a particularly interesting example of this effect can be found in a recent study of congressional voting on the tariff. Hall, Kao and Nelson rely on historical accounts to show that women were perceived as preferring a low tariff because higher tariffs raised the prices of their household purchases. In the language of economics, "each household is seen as having a wealth effect voter and a consumption effect voter." Comparing the theoretical tariff equilibria under voting by men only vs. voting by both men and women, the authors hypothesize that including women in the voting universe lowers the equilibrium tariff. Empirically, analyzing the tariff from 1890 to 1934, they find a strong effect,

47. Muncy, *Creating a Female Dominion,* 152.
48. Sklar, "Historical Foundations of Women's Power," 75.
49. Lemons, *The Woman Citizen,* 111.

with female enfranchisement lowering the tariff (as do Democratic presidents and unemployment). The authors conclude that "female franchise had a statistically significant effect on a fundamental political issue of the time." More important for the present argument, these authors dismiss the arguments that "all women didn't vote" or that "many women didn't vote." Men and women in the 1920s, they argue, "were presumed to disagree" about the tariff. Furthermore, political science research suggests that "people need not vote to be considered in the political calculus of re-election maximizing politicians, they only need to be able to vote."[50] Certainly this is consistent with the views of men and women in the 1920s. As I mentioned in chapter 2, woman suffrage put pressure on Congress to pass legislation protecting women's citizenship—legislation that had "no force" before ratification of the Nineteenth Amendment. Similarly, Florence Allen (at the time justice of the Ohio Supreme Court) wrote in evaluating woman suffrage that "whether or not the ballot is exercised at all . . . there is a potential power in the franchise which makes its holder more influential than the one who does not have the vote." Before 1920, she went on, whether women complained about local problems or broader issues, "their protests for the most part fell upon deaf ears. They spoke not with the voice of the master, but with the voice of the pleader. This has vastly altered since 1920."[51]

CHANGING WOMEN AND CHANGING POLITICS

In 1923 John W. Burgess, who set up the first graduate program in political science at Columbia, expressed his reservations about suffrage, arguing that "the great enterprises of voluntary socialism have been carried forward in this country more by women than by men. It has been preeminently their sphere of communal action. . . . while

50. H. Keith Hall, Chihwa Kao and Douglas Nelson, "Women and Tariffs: Testing the Gender Gap Hypothesis in a Downs-Mayer Political Economy Model." Even now, in the age of omnipresent polling, it is not always possible to predict which population groups will vote and which will not. Before suffrage, politicians had no real reason to "value the support or fear the opposition of voteless citizens" (Kraditor 1965: 220), but after suffrage a politician would have been foolish to base his actions on the expectation of low voter turnout among women.

51. Allen, "The First Ten Years."

politics and government have been left for the men."[52] Similarly, the
views of Walter Lippmann in 1928 reflect the stereotype of moralistic
(and therefore nonpolitical) women—a stereotype that continued to
appear in many social science accounts up to and including the 1960s
and 1970s.[53] According to Lippmann, women concentrate on "moral
issues" because they have not had executive experience. The moral
concerns divert their attention from the "central issues" in politics.
"They prevent women in politics from centering their attention on
those questions of power and privilege which are the real subject
matter of government."[54]

But any recent historical description of women's activities in the
late nineteenth and early twentieth centuries makes clear that
women played a critical role, even before suffrage, in transforming
the political system. Kathryn Kish Sklar, for example, in a recent es-
say claims correctly that "All [historians] have agreed that women
were central to the process by which the American social contract
was recast and state and federal governments assumed greater responsibility for human welfare."[55] From our standpoint many years
later, we can plainly see that the efforts of women's voluntary associations, women's lobbying, and the "female dominion" *did* help to
transform politics and government. But however we define politics
today—say, for example, that we use David Easton's definition that
politics is the authoritative allocation of values—we are likely to define the term much more broadly than Americans in the 1920s did.
For many of them (like Lippmann and Burgess), women were simply
"defined out" of what *they* thought of as politics.[56]

52. Barbara J. Nelson, "Crossing the Borders: Women and the Boundaries of
Knowledge in Political Science," 5 (my italics).
53. Susan C. Bourque and Jean Grossholtz, "Politics an Unnatural Practice:
Political Science Looks at Female Participation," *Politics and Society* 4 (1974),
225–66.
54. Walter Lippmann, "Lady Politicians: How the Old-Fashioned Illusion That
Women would Redeem Politics Has Been Destroyed," *Vanity Fair* 29 (January
1928), 104
55. Sklar, "Historical Foundations of Women's Power," 44.
56. Naomi Black, in *Social Feminism* (Ithaca: Cornell University Press, 1989),
242–43, discusses the common criticism made of the League of Women Voters for
being "nonpartisan" and therefore "nonpolitical". The criticisms of the League are
very much like the quotes from Lane, Easton and Dennis, and so on which Bourque
and Grossholtz cite in "Politics an Unnatural Practice": if women are interested in
it, it's not political or sophisticated.

Here is a concrete example. In 1908, Belle Israels (later Moskowitz) organized a committee of members of the Council of Jewish
Women to study "working girls' leisure" and, eventually, to push for
the regulation of dance halls and other amusements which were
thought to encourage promiscuity and associated social evils. Over
the next few years this committee conducted extensive surveys of
public amusements in New York City, enlarged the committee to
include many influential citizens, publicized problems with dance
halls through articles, combined public and private funds to create
"model" dance halls, and successfully sponsored state and municipal
legislation regulating and licensing dance halls.[57] Today we would
say that she had been actively working in local and state politics, but
in 1912, what she and other women were could not be considered
politics because it was women's work and therefore nonpolitical.
Some women did try to change the way politics was conceptualized.
Mrs. Henry Ridgely, president of Delaware State League of Women
Voters, spoke at that League's convention in 1920: "We have been
unused to the word politics applied to women's activities. Don't let
us shun it because it is strange or because it has been associated with
partisanship, with group hatred and distrust, . . . Look at it clearly—
say it distinctly. Politics, women in politics, and then consider what
it means. . . . Politics does not mean, should not mean, partisanship.
I think it is because voters have allowed demagogues and bosses—or
special interests—to loom so big that they entirely obscure moral
issues; that the term political argument, political measure, has come
to mean to us some partisan argument, some special interest measure."[58] But both men and women resisted the idea of changing or
broadening the conventional understanding of politics. Even in 1925,
Emily Newell Blair described women's organizations as "nonpolitical" as long as politics consisted of explicitly partisan and/or electoral
activities. "To the average person today [politics] . . . means attending
conventions, choosing nominees, and possibly electing them." Marguerite Wells agreed: "Politics to most people means party politics."[59]

57. Perry, *Belle Moskowitz*, ch. 3.
58. *Woman Citizen,* 9 October 1920, 509, 512.
59. Blair, "Are Women a Failure in Politics?" Wells, "Some Effects of Woman
Suffrage."

In this book I have described women's discussions of their obligations as citizens as well as their attempts to secure important positions within the parties and to gain elective offices. In doing so I have tried to portray the distinction between male and female political cultures and the resistance of male political elites to women's entry into the male domain of politics. From our perspective seventy years later, both men and women in 1920 were involved in politics, but they were using different political forms and strategies. From the perspective of 1920, however, politics was defined much more narrowly: traditionally, only men did politics.

The gender boundaries defining behavior in the public arena shifted during the 1920s. As more and more women voted, campaigns, balloting, and even the polling places themselves began to lose their association with men, male rituals and masculine virtues. As more women ran for and won public office, Americans' notions of what a politician looked like and acted like changed. But almost all women who became active in the parties or who ran for office had their formative political experiences in a distinctive female political culture.[60] Such women saw themselves as having political interests and skills fundamentally different from those of men. Thus the boundary had shifted to include not just *women,* but aspects of a female political culture. Women's exclusion from electoral politics, and their extensive work in voluntary organizations as well as in the suffrage movement, created a distinct political style, which might be generally described as based on cooperation, gathering information, and building consensus. Anne Scott argues that women's separatist experience, in women's organizations and associations, had a particular effect: "Women learned to be professionals before the traditional professions were open to them, and developed a recognizable female style of professional behavior that relied heavily on cooperation. Reflecting their voluntary-association training, the first women doctors, lawyers, teachers, and ministers often functioned differently from their male counterparts." Muncy also concludes that because of their distinct assumptions and professional values, women in policymaking positions often created programs different from those men would have developed.

60. Ware, *Beyond Suffrage.*

Women's "natural" characteristics of gentleness and caring were sometimes seen as rendering them unfit for the rigors of "real" politics. Eleanor Roosevelt said that "In the old days men always said that politics was too rough-and-tumble a business for women; but that idea is gradually wearing away." Was it "wearing away" because women in politics were changing, adapting to the male-defined norms of the partisan and electoral arenas? Ruth McCormick, pictured on the cover of *Time* when she ran for the Senate in 1928 over the caption "she learned the law of the jungle," is an interesting case in this context. Like other women who were active in politics in the 1920s, her experiences within the male world of politics had a strong influence; like these women, her political socialization took place, in effect, in the "wrong sphere." Kristie Miller's recent biography of McCormick makes this clear:

> Ruth was now sixteen, and was being indoctrinated into
> old-fashioned partisan campaigning. She loved the
> drama of nineteenth-century popular politics. "It was
> the ambition of my life," she later recalled, "to walk in a
> torchlight parade. When I was finally permitted to, I
> walked until my legs nearly fell off. I screamed and
> yelled until my throat was sore. I waved the torch until
> it dripped on me and my face was black and burned."
> At this point it would be well to remember that most
> women of her time were never initiated into the prevail-
> ing political culture; twenty-five years later [1920] it
> would be hard for them to participate in politics as men
> of their age would easily do.[61]

When she was sixteen, McCormick went to Washington with her father, who had been appointed to fill out a Senate term, and acted as his confidential secretary. "When Hanna was in commit-tee, he delegated Ruth to sit in the Senate gallery and report to him what happened in debate, as well as the attitude of certain senators to questions under discussion. She learned legislative pro-cedure, as well as the political technique of the Capitol, for exam-

61. Miller, *Ruth Hanna McCormick*, 17.

ple, how a bill gets on and off the calendar. And she learned to love the drama of debate."[62] McCormick was straightforwardly politically ambitious in the traditional "male" way—as Belle Moskowitz and many others were not. She loved campaigning and "politicking," wanted to win, and saw herself as unusual (because she was a woman candidate when there were few) but much like other politicians. She was one of the rare women in the 1920s who, in fact, described herself as a politician.[63]

Even Ruth McCormick, however, thought of women has having some distinct political attributes. She pointed out that women working for suffrage "did not see that it was necessary to seek advice and learn the ways of politics from experienced politicians" but had in effect developed their own methods. Thus rather than sit patiently at the feet of male mentors, she proposed that women "bring their fresh enthusiasms, their distinctive viewpoints, and their quick instincts into cooperation with men's longer experience" in order to form a "power partnership."[64] McCormick, like Emily Newell Blair, Eleanor Roosevelt, and other women active in partisan politics, continued to think that there were persisting differences in political style. "There is more truth," Roosevelt said, "in the statement that men have a different attitude toward politics than women. They play politics a little more like a game. With the men, it becomes a serious occupation for a few weeks before election; whereas women look upon it as a serious matter year in and year out. It is associated with their patriotism and their duty to their country."[65] This statement is interesting in that it clearly implies that the community-based or "municipal housekeeping" work that women had been doing for a long time—"year in and year out," as Roosevelt says—has now come under the rubric of

62. Miller, *Ruth Hanna McCormick,* 21.

63. Similarly, Pennsylvanian Cornelia Bryce Pinchot said in 1925 that "you must remember that I was a politician . . . before I ever met Mr. Pinchot." She had grown up in a political family, like Ruth Hanna; Teddy Roosevelt was a family friend. Based on her experience, she was convinced that "politics is the best of all indoor sports." Furlow, "Cornelia Bryce Pinchot," quotes from 330 and 338.

64. Miller, *Ruth Hanna McCormick,* 129.

65. Eleanor Roosevelt, "Women in Politics," *Good Housekeeping* 110 (January 1940), 19.

politics. We can find other illustrations of what seems to be a change in the way women in electoral and party politics expanded the boundaries of "the political." Lillian Wald, founder of the Henry Street Settlement in New York, said later "When I went to New York, and was stirred to participate in community work . . . I believed that politics concerned itself with matters outside [women's] realm and experience. It was an awakening to me to realize that when I was working in the interests of those babies . . . I was really in politics."[66]

When women gained suffrage, and when along with the constitutional change came new party rules and more women in campaigns and public office, the question of "who does politics?" required a new answer. In response, men in parties tried to redefine politics so that women's activities and interests were clearly distinguished from men's: as a result, the space occupied by "real" (male) politics constricted. We have seen how this happened repeatedly: when judges ruled that the right to hold office did not accompany the right to vote, or when the chairman of the Democratic National Committee expressed surprise that the new women members of the DNC might actually want to participate in its decision-making. But this redefinition did not really work, because women protested the constraints in many ways. They tried to negotiate changes in the rules to give women more power, and they often refused to be bound by stereotypical ideas of how women should behave or what women's interests were.

And once women were in politics, despite their very limited power, they brought with them the concerns and issues that had animated women's work for years. In fact, women were seen (and mostly saw themselves) as having little political ambition in the conventional sense (see chapter 5) but rather as being principally motivated by issue-based concerns. The sorts of legislation that individual women legislators and women's groups supported in the 1920s is evidence of the continuity of the women's agenda.[67] It makes sense, then, to suggest that as the answer to "who does

66. Doris Daniels, "Building a Winning Coalition: The Suffrage Fight in New York State," *New York History* 60 (1979), 67–68.

67. Lemons, *The Woman Citizen;* Cott, "Across the Great Divide"; Johnson, "Organized Women Lobbyists."

politics?" changed, the answer to "what is politics?" changed also, as the quotations from Eleanor Roosevelt and Lillian Wald illustrate. Writing in 1940, Eleanor Roosevelt described the important work of women in FDR's administration, and concluded that although women have voted as individuals, dividing in the same ways as men, she saw a connection between women's vote and the fact that "on the whole, during the last 20 years, government has been taking increasing cognizance of humanitarian questions, things that deal with the happiness of human beings, such as health, education, and security."[68]

At the same time, activist women now saw politics from the inside, closer to the "numbra" that Carrie Chapman Catt had described to them, and were often uneasy with the stated and unstated norms of partisan politics. While male party leaders may have been "shocked rather often by women voters who, while engaged loyally in their party duties, have questioned the method or the wisdom of the process,"[69] those women who gained real political power and influence adapted to those norms, accepting as given the existing system of partisanship and patronage. Again, most women were not personally ambitious: their own ideas about gender did not support ambition, and as Muncy argues, women had historically worked to create social change through their own professions and their own professional networks in a different way than conventional political change took place. The notion of clashing interests, of "winners" and "losers," was anathema to many women (although Ruth McCormick was clearly an exception). Eventually, women who condemned patronage and sought involvement in high politics were forced to adapt to reality, though of course the importance of patronage as an incentive for ensuring party loyalty was declining sharply in the 1930s. By the time of the New Deal, opposition to patronage had largely evaporated.

> The dominion could no longer have been said to exist
> after 1935 because so many women themselves won

68. Eleanor Roosevelt, "Women in Politics," *Good Housekeeping* 110 (March 1940), 45.

69. Carrie Chapman Catt, "What Women Have Done with the Vote," *Independent* 115 (17 October 1925), 447.

their highest positions in the federal bureaucracy through patronage appointments by Franklin Roosevelt. Prior to Roosevelt's presidency, female leaders had exercised tight control over jobs within the child welfare network. Because these women had held themselves aloof from partisan politics and convinced successive Presidents that patronage should not dictate their hiring, female leaders had been able to draw through their own institutions younger women who mirrored their values and strategies for public policy. During the 1930s, this changed: most of the women who achieved high office did so especially because they had campaigned for Roosevelt's election.[70]

In other words, women had changed, but so had the "tiger." Women had entered more fully into electoral and partisan politics, and though gendered boundaries remained, they had shifted considerably. Women were voters, county treasurers, heads of federal agencies, and for the most part they retained the attributes that had previously defined them out of politics. In this way they brought their particular experiences, political strategies, and political styles into the traditionally male domain of partisan and electoral politics, and in doing so began to slowly change how that politics was conceptualized. Passages from two books about politics illustrate this change. In *Common Sense in Politics* (1910), Job Hedges writes, "The number of federal questions of recent years have been reasonably limited and confined to the tariff, finance, internal improvements, foreign relations, and such typical topics. The expansion of business . . . has emphasized the necessity for exercising federal authority under the Constitution in the matter of inter-state commerce.[71]

These are the "central issues," the "real subject matter" of male politics that Lippmann referred to. Reflecting this, in the 1916 *New York Times Index*, only eight percent of the stories about congressional bills referred to bills which did not easily fall into

70. Muncy, *Creating a Female Dominion*, 155.
71. Job E. Hedges, *Common Sense in Politics* (New York: Moffat, Yard & Co., 1910), 18–19.

Mr. Hedges' categories, and over half of this small amount had to do with immigration. The child labor bill was covered, as was a bill to appropriate money for vocational education. In contrast, Pendleton Herring, in his classic *The Politics of Democracy* (1940), wrote that "The development of accepted standards of proper administration plus agreement on social goals has shifted the realization of many public policies from the realm of partisan conflict. This means, for example, that a sufficiently powerful combination of interests is in agreement on the desirability of parks and public recreation facilities and on the means best suited to this goal. Today politicians may sponsor social services within broad limits without damaging their respectability in the eyes of middle-class voters. Relief and social services even emerge as basic objectives in framing public policy."[72]

Women's entrance into party and electoral politics in the 1920s was part of a slow process of shifting boundaries that continues today. The changes that took place in the decade after suffrage had important implications for the way that citizenship and gender were related; for the national policy agenda; and as one of the processes that contributed to the end of the "party era." For the first time, women's inclusion in the public sphere was not *only* through their private lives but was direct and (potentially) self-interested rather than selfless. When women voted, the myth of indirectness was preserved by the idea that women "voted like their husbands." When women held office, the myth of disinterestedness was preserved by the idea that women were in politics for the sake of their families or communities. That these illusions were not totally convincing is suggested by the extent to which male political elites resisted women's ambitions and demands. Women's relationship to the public sphere is still mediated by family; liberal democratic theory's insistence on a world of free and equal individuals is, consequently, fundamentally flawed.[73] But the achievement of suffrage and the direct experience of women in politics during the twenties—as voters, party activists, candidates, and office-

72. Pendleton Herring, *The Politics of Democracy* (New York: W. W. Norton, 1940), 29.

73. Susan Muller Okin, *Justice, Gender and the Family* (New York: Basic Books, 1991).

holders—brought into question the notion that women could (or should) have only an indirect relationship to public discourse and public decision-making.

Women voters behaved—or were perceived to behave, which is just as important—more independently than men. Not surprisingly, their party loyalties were less established, and certainly suffragists' experiences with the major parties had imbued them with skepticism toward both Democrats and Republicans. Women were also perceived by party leaders, journalists, and the general public to be potentially, if not operationally, a distinct group: to have a distinct policy agenda and distinct policy preferences. The parties acted on this assumption when they acted in specific contexts to mobilize women. Despite the fact that this potentiality seemed less and less likely to be used as the decade wore on, I believe that woman suffrage did have an impact on political decision-making and on the shape of the political agenda. This was so both because the reconstituted electorate necessitated a changed calculus and because visible women in the parties and in public office were able to use their connections with women reformers to preserve, if only partially and precariously, the progressive impulse through the unfriendly twenties. At the same time, the new women voters' greater independence from party, combined with innovations like the League of Women Voters' candidate surveys and debates, the transformation of the act of voting from a male ritual to a good citizen's obligation, and the organizational innovations pioneered by women's groups, helped to solidify the movement from the partisan-structured politics of the nineteenth century to the politics of advertising, interest groups, and candidates that characterize the twentieth century.

BIBLIOGRAPHY

Adams, Mildred. "What Are Women Mayors Doing?" *American City* 26 (June 1922): 543–44.
———. *The Right to Be People.* Philadelphia: J. B. Lippincott, 1967.
Addams, Jane. *Democracy and Social Ethics.* Ed. Ann Firor Scott. 1902. Reprint, Cambridge: Harvard University Press, 1964.
Allen, Florence E. "The First Ten Years." *Woman's Journal,* August 1930, pp. 5–7, 30–32.
———. "Participation of Women in Government." *Annals of the American Academy of Political and Social Science* 251 (May 1947): 94–110.
Alpern, Sara, and Dale Baum. "Female Ballots: The Impact of the Nineteenth Amendment." *Journal of Interdisciplinary History* 16 (summer 1986): 43–67.
Andersen, Kristi. *The Creation of a Democratic Majority, 1928–1936.* Chicago: University of Chicago Press, 1979.
———. "Women and Citizenship in the 1920s." In *Women, Politics, and Change.* Ed. Louise A. Tilly and Patricia Gurin. New York: Russell Sage Foundation, 1990.
———. "Women and the Vote in the 1920s: What Happened in Oregon." *Women and Politics* 14, no. 4 (1994): 43–56.
Anderson, George E. "Women in Congress." *Commonweal* 9 (13 March 1929): 532–534.
Arneson, Ben A. "Non-Voting in a Typical Ohio Community." *American Political Science Review* 19 (1925): 816–25.
Baer, Denise L. "Political Parties: The Missing Variable in Women and Politics Research." *Political Research Quarterly* 46 (1993): 567–75.
Baker, Paula. "The Domestication of Politics: Women and American Political Society, 1780–1920." *American Historical Review* 89 (June 1984): 620–47.
———. *The Moral Frameworks of Public Life: Gender, Politics, and the State in Rural New York, 1870–1930.* New York: Oxford, 1991.
Barber, Benjamin. *Strong Democracy.* Berkeley: University of California Press, 1984.
Barnard, Eunice Fuller. "The Woman Voter Gains Power." *New York Times Magazine,* 12 August 1928, pp. 1–3, 20.

————. "Women Who Wield Political Power." *New York Times Magazine,* 2 September 1928, pp. 6–7, 23.

————. "Women in the Campaign." *Woman's Journal,* December 1928, pp. 7–9, 44–45.

Baxter, Sandra, and Marjorie Lansing. *Women and Politics: The Invisible Majority.* Ann Arbor: University of Michigan Press, 1980.

Beck, Paul Allen. "A Socialization Theory of Partisan Realignment." In *Controversies in American Voting Behavior.* Ed. Richard Niemi and Herbert Weisberg. San Francisco: W. H. Freeman, 1976.

Becker, Susan D. *The Origins of the Equal Rights Amendment: American Feminism between the Wars.* Westport, CT: Greenwood Press, 1981.

Beckwith, Karen. "The Public-Private Distinction and Why Women Can't Be Citizens." Paper presented at the meetings of the Midwest Political Science Association, Cincinnati, OH, 1981.

Bendix, John. "Women's Suffrage and Political Culture: A Modern Swiss Case." *Women and Politics* 12, no. 3 (1992): 27–56.

Berry, Jeffrey M. 1977. *Lobbying for the People: The Political Behavior of Public Interest Groups.* Princeton: Princeton University Press, 1977.

Black, Naomi. *Social Feminism.* Ithaca: Cornell University Press, 1989.

Blair, Emily Newell. "Are Women a Failure in Politics?" *Harpers Magazine* 151 (June-November 1925): 513–22.

————. "Men in Politics as a Woman Sees Them." *Harpers Magazine* 152 (May 1926): 703–9.

————. "Women in the Political Parties." *Annals of the American Academy of Political Science* 143 (1929): 217–29.

————. "Wanted—A New Feminism." Interview by Mary Carroll. *Independent Woman* 9 (December 1930), pp. 499, 544.

————. "Why I Am Discouraged About Women in Politics." *Woman's Journal,* January 1931, pp. 20–22.

Blair, Karen J. *The Clubwoman as Feminist: True Womanhood Redefined, 1868–1914.* New York: Homes and Meier, 1980.

Bourque, Susan C. and Jean Grossholtz. "Politics an Unnatural Practice: Political Science Looks at Female Participation." *Politics and Society* 4 (1974): 225–66.

Breckinridge, Sophonisba P. "The Activities of Women Outside the Home." In *Recent Social Trends in the United States.* Report of the President's Research Committee on Social Trends. New York: McGraw-Hill, 1933.

————. *Women in the Twentieth Century.* New York: McGraw-Hill, 1933.

Brown, Courtney. *Ballots of Tumult: A Portrait of Volatility in American Voting.* Ann Arbor: University of Michigan Press, 1991.

Brown, Dorothy M. *Mabel Walker Willebrandt: A Study of Power, Loyalty, and Law.* Knoxville: University of Tennessee Press, 1984.

————. "Power in Washington: Networking in the 1920s from Willebrandt to Roosevelt." Paper presented at the Conference on Women, Politics and Change, New School for Social Research, New York, NY, April 1990.

Brumbaugh, Sara B. "Democratic Experience and Education in the League of Women Voters." Ph.D. thesis, Columbia University, 1946.

Buenker, John D. *Urban Liberalism and Progressive Reform*. New York: Scribners, 1973.

Burner, David. *The Politics of Provincialism: The Democratic Party in Transition, 1918–1932*. New York: W. W. Norton, 1967.

Burnham, Walter Dean. "The Changing Shape of the American Political Universe." *American Political Science Review* 59 (March 1965): 7–28.

———. "Theory and Voting Research: Some Reflections on Converse's 'Change in the American Electorate.'" *American Political Science Review* 68 (1974): 1002–23.

———. "The System of 1896: An Analysis." In *The Evolution of American Electoral Systems*. Ed. Paul Kleppner, et. al. Westport, CT: Greenwood Press, 1981.

Burton, Robert E. *Democrats of Oregon: The Pattern of Minority Politics, 1900–1956*. Eugene: University of Oregon Press, 1970.

Butler, Sarah Schuyler. "Women Who Do Not Vote." *Scribner's Magazine* 76 (November 1924): 529–33.

———. "After Ten Years." *Woman's Journal*, April 1929, pp. 10–11.

CJD. "The Nineteenth Amendment As Affecting the Right of Women to Hold Public Office." *Temple Law Quarterly* 2 (April 1928): 278–79.

Catt, Carrie Chapman. "Political Parties and Women Voters." Address delivered to the Congress of the League of Women Voters, Chicago, 14 February 1920. Women's Rights Collection, Box 56, F747, Schlesinger Library.

———. "A Teapot in a Tempest." *Woman Citizen*, 5 February 1921.

———. "What Women Have Done with the Vote." *Independent* 115 (17 October 1925): 447–48, 456.

Chafe, William. *The American Woman: Her Changing Social, Economic and Political Roles, 1920–1970*. New York: Oxford University Press, 1972.

Chambers, Clark A. *Seedtime of Reform*. Minneapolis: University of Minnesota Press, 1963.

Claggett, William. "The Life Cycle and Generational Models of the Development of Partisanship: A Test Based on the Delayed Enfranchisement of Women." *Social Science Quarterly* 60 (1980): 643–50.

Claggett, William, and John Van Wingen. "Conversion and Recruitment in Boston during the New Deal Realignment: A Preliminary Comparison of Men and Women." Paper presented at the Southern Political Science Association annual meeting, Atlanta, GA, November 1990.

Clark, Ida Clyde. "Feminists Made Gains in Many Fields in 1928." *New York Times*, 17 February 1929, p. 8.

Clemens, Elisabeth S. "Organizational Repertoires and Institutional

Change: Women's Groups and the Transformation of U.S. Politics, 1890–1920." *American Journal of Sociology* 98 (January 1993): 755–98.

Converse, Philip E. "Of Time and Partisan Stability." *Comparative Political Studies* 2 (July 1969): 139–71.

———. "Change in the American Electorate." In *The Human Meaning of Social Change.* Ed. Angus Campbell and Philip E. Converse. New York: Russell Sage, 1972.

———. *The Dynamics of Party Support: Cohort Analyzing Party Identification.* Beverly Hills: Sage Publications, 1976.

Cook, Blanche Weisen. "Female Support Networks and Political Activism: Lillian Wald, Crystal Eastman, Emma Goldman." In *A Heritage of Her Own: Toward a New Social History of Women.* Ed. Nancy F. Cott and Elizabeth H. Pleck. New York: Simon and Schuster, 1979.

Costin, Lela. *Two Sisters for Social Justice: A Biography of Grace and Edith Abbott.* Urbana: University of Illinois Press, 1983.

Cott, Nancy. "Feminist Politics in the 1920s: The National Woman's Party." *Journal of American History* 71 (1984): 43–68.

———. *The Grounding of Modern Feminism.* New Haven: Yale University Press, 1987.

———. "Across the Great Divide: Women in Politics Before and After 1920." In *Women, Politics, and Change.* Ed. Louise A. Tilly and Patricia Gurin. New York: Russell Sage Foundation, 1990: 153–76.

Daniels, Doris. "Building a Winning Coalition: The Suffrage Fight in New York State." *New York History* 60 (1979): 58–80.

Darcy, R., Susan Welch, and Janet Clark. *Women, Elections, and Representation.* New York: Longman Press, 1987.

David, Paul T., Ralph M. Goldman, and Richard C. Bain. *The Politics of National Party Conventions.* Washington, D.C.: Brookings Institution, 1960.

Degler, Carl N. *At Odds: Women and the Family in America from the Revolution to the Present.* New York: Oxford University Press, 1980.

Democratic National Committee. *Women's Democratic Campaign Manual.* Washington, D.C.: Democratic National Committee and Democratic Congressional Committee, 1924.

Deutsch, Sarah. "Learning to Talk More Like a Man: Boston Women's Class-Bridging Organizations, 1870–1940." *American Historical Review* 97 (April 1992): 379–404.

Diggins, John Patrick. "Republicanism and Progressivism." *American Quarterly* 37 (fall 1985): 572–98.

Dobyns, Winifred Starr. "The Lady and the Tiger." *Woman Citizen,* January 1927, pp. 20–21, 44–45.

Dodson, Debra, and Susan Carroll. *Reshaping the Agenda: Women in State Legislatures.* New Brunswick, NJ: Center for the American Woman and Politics, Rutgers University, 1991.

Douglas, Ann. *The Feminization of American Culture*. New York: Knopf, 1977.

DuBois, Ellen Carol. *Feminism and Suffrage: The Emergence of an Independent Women's Movement in America, 1848–1869*. Ithaca: Cornell University Press, 1978.

Elshtain, Jean Bethke. *Public Man, Private Woman*. Princeton: Princeton University Press, 1981.

Fenno, Richard. *Home Style*. Boston: Little, Brown and Co., 1978.

Filene, Peter G. "An Obituary for the Progressive Movement." *American Quarterly* 22 (1970): 20–34.

Fisher, Marguerite J. "Women in the Political Parties." *The Annals of the American Academy of Political and Social Science* 251 (May 1947): 87–93.

Fisher, Marguerite J., and Betty Whitehead. "Women and National Party Organization." *American Political Science Review* 38 (1944): 895–903.

Fitzpatrick, Ellen. *Endless Crusade: Women Social Scientists and Progressive Reform*. New York: Oxford University Press, 1990.

Flanagan, Maureen A. "Gender and Urban Political Reform: The City Club and the Woman's City Club of Chicago in the Progressive Era." *American Historical Review* 95 (October 1990): 1032–50.

Flexner, Eleanor. *Century of Struggle: The Woman's Rights Movement in the United States*. New York: Athenaeum, 1974.

Flexner, Helen Thomas. Introduction to *Equal Suffrage* by Helen L. Sumner. New York: Harper & Brothers, 1909.

Fowler, Linda L. and Robert D. McClure. *Political Ambition*. New Haven: Yale University Press, 1989.

Fowler, Robert Booth. *Carrie Catt: Feminist Politician*. Boston: Northeastern University Press, 1986.

Frankel, Noralee and Nancy S. Dye, eds. *Gender, Class, Race and Reform in the Progressive Era*. Lexington: University Press of Kentucky, 1991.

Freedman, Estelle B. "The New Woman: Changing Views of Women in the 1920s." *Journal of American History* 61 (September 1974): 372–84.

———. "Separatism as Strategy: Female Institution Building and American Feminism, 1870–1930." *Feminist Studies* 5 (1979): 512–29.

Furlow, John W., Jr. "Cornelia Bryce Pinchot: Feminism in the Post-Suffrage Era." *Pennsylvania History* 43 (October 1976): 329–46.

Gamm, Gerald. *The Making of New Deal Democrats: Voting Behavior and Realignment in Boston, 1920–1940*. Chicago: University of Chicago Press, 1986.

Gehlen, Frieda L. "Women Members of Congress: A Distinctive Role." In *A Portrait of Marginality: The Political Behavior of the American Woman*. Ed. Marianne Githens and Jewel L. Prestage New York: David McKay, 1977.

Gerould, Katherine F. "Some American Women and the Vote." *Scribner's Magazine* 77 (May 1925): 449–52.

Gerson, Judith M., and Kathy Peiss. "Boundaries, Negotiation, Conscious-
    ness: Reconceptualizing Gender Relations." *Social Problems* 32, no. 4
    (1985): 317–31.

Getis, Victoria. 1993. "Doing the Work of Government: The Chicago
    Woman's Club and Progressive Reform." Paper presented at the meet-
    ing of the Social Science History Association, Baltimore, MD, Novem-
    ber 1993.

Gienapp, William E. "Politics Seems to Enter Into Everything." In *Essays
    on Antebellum Politics, 1840–1860.* Ed. S. E. Maizlish and J. J. Kushma.
    College Station: Texas A & M Press, 1982

Glenn, Norval C. "Sources of the Shift to Political Independence: Some
    Evidence from a Cohort Analysis." *Social Science Quarterly* 37 (spring
    1972): 1–20.

Goldstein, Joel H. "The Effects of the Adoption of Woman Suffrage:
    Sex Differences in Voting Behavior—Illinois, 1914–1921." Ph.D. thesis,
    University of Chicago, 1973.

Good, Josephine L. *Republican Womanpower: The History of Women in
    Republican National Conventions and Women in the Republican Na-
    tional Committee.* Washington, D.C.: Republican National Committee,
    1963.

Gordon, Felice D. "After Winning: The New Jersey Suffragists, 1910–
    1947." Ph.D. thesis, Rutgers University of the State University of New
    Jersey, 1982.

———. *After Winning: The Legacy of the New Jersey Suffragists, 1920–
    1947.* New Brunswick: Rutgers University Press, 1986.

Green, Elizabeth. "I Resign from Female Politics." *New Republic* 42 (22
    April 1925): 234–35.

Grinnell, Katherine. *Woman's Place in Government.* New York: Bicker-
    dike and Winegard, 1917.

Gruberg, Martin. *Women in American Politics.* Oshkosh, WI: Academia
    Press, 1968.

Gullett, Gayle. "City Mothers, City Daughters, and the Dance Hall Girls:
    The Limits of Female Political Power in San Francisco, 1913." In
    Women and the Structure of Society. Ed. Barbara J. Harris and JoAnn
    K. McNamara. Durham, NC: Duke University Press, 1984.

Gustafson, Melanie. "The Women of 1912: The Struggle for Inclusion in
    the Political Parties." Paper presented at the Organization of American
    Historians Meetings, Atlanta, GA, April 1994.

Harbaugh, William M. "The Republican Party, 1893–1932." In *History of
    U.S. Political Parties,* 3. Ed. Arthur M. Schlesinger, Jr. New York: Chel-
    sea House, 1963.

Harvey, Anna. "Uncertain Victory: The Electoral Incorporation of Women
    into the Republican Party, 1920–1928." Paper presented at the Ameri-
    can Political Science Association meetings, Washington, D.C., 1992.

Hays, Samuel P. "Political Parties and the Community-Society Continuum." In *The American Party Systems*. Ed. William Nisbet Chambers and Walter Dean Burnham. New York: Oxford, 1967.

Hedges, Job E. *Common Sense in Politics*. New York: Moffat, Yard & Co, 1910.

Herring, Pendleton. *The Politics of Democracy*. New York: W. W. Norton, 1940.

Higginbotham, Evelyn Brooks. "In Politics to Stay: Black Women Leaders and Party Politics in the 1920s." In *Women, Politics, and Change*. Ed. Louise A. Tilly and Patricia Gurin. New York: Russell Sage Foundation, 1990.

Hummer, Patricia M. *The Decade of Elusive Promise: Professional Women in the United States, 1920–1930*. Ann Arbor: UMI Research Press, 1979.

Huus, Randolph O. "Cleveland Women in Government and Allied Fields." *National Municipal Review* 19 (1930): 88–92.

Jablonsky, Thomas J. "Duty, Nature, and Stability: The Female Anti-Suffragists in the United States, 1894–1920." Ph.D. thesis, University of California at Los Angeles, 1978.

Jennings, M. Kent. "Women in Party Politics." In *Women, Politics, and Change*. Ed. Louise A. Tilly and Patricia Gurin. New York: Russell Sage Foundation, 1990.

Jensen, Joan M. " 'Disfranchisement Is a Disgrace': Women and Politics in New Mexico, 1900–1940." *New Mexico Historical Review* 56 (January 1981): 5–35

———. "All Pink Sisters: The War Department and the Feminist Movement in the 1920s." In *Decades of Discontent*. Ed. Lois Scharf and Joan Jensen. Westport, CT: Greenwood Press, 1983.

Jensen, Richard. *The Winning of the Midwest*. Chicago: University of Chicago Press, 1971.

Jerrard, Margot. "Emily Newell Blair." In *Notable American Women: The Modern Period*. Ed. Barbara Sicherman. Cambridge: Harvard University Press, 1980.

Johnson, Dorothy. "Organized Women as Lobbyists in the 1920s." *Capitol Studies* 1 (1972): 41–58.

Jones, Jacqueline. "The Political Implications of Black and White Women's Work in the South, 1890–1965." In *Women, Politics, and Change*. Ed. Louise A. Tilly and Patricia Gurin, New York: Russell Sage Foundation, 1990.

Jordan, Jean P. "Women Merchants in Colonial New York." *New York History* 58 (October 1977): 412–39.

Kenton, Edna. "Four Years of Equal Suffrage." *Forum* 72 (July 1924): 37–44.

Kerber, Linda K. *Women of the Republic: Intellect and Ideology in Revolutionary America*. Chapel Hill: University of North Carolina Press, 1980.

———. "The Republican Ideology of the Revolutionary Generation." *American Quarterly* 37 (fall 1985): 474–95.

———. "Separate Spheres, Female Worlds, Woman's Place: The Rhetoric of Women's History." *Journal of American History* 75 (June 1988): 9–39.

Key, V. O. *American State Politics: An Introduction.* New York: Alfred A. Knopf, 1956.

Kingdon, John. *Congressmen's Voting Decisions.* New York: Harper & Row, 1973.

Kleppner, Paul. "Were Women to Blame? Female Suffrage and Voter Turnout." *Journal of Interdisciplinary History* 12 (spring 1982): 621–43.

Koch, Raymond L. "Politics and Relief in Minneapolis during the 1930s." *Minnesota History* 41 (1968): 153–70.

Kraditor, Aileen S. *The Ideas of the Woman Suffrage Movement, 1890–1920.* New York: Columbia University Press, 1965.

Ladd-Taylor, Molly. "Hull House Goes to Washington: Women and the Children's Bureau." In *Gender, Class, Race, and Reform in the Progressive Era.* Ed. Noralee Frankel and Nancy S. Dye. Lexington: University Press of Kentucky, 1991.

Lebsock, Suzanne. "Women and American Politics, 1880–1920." In *Women Politics and Change.* Ed. Louise A. Tilly and Patricia Gurin. New York: Russell Sage Foundation, 1990.

Lee, Marcia M. "Why Few Women Hold Public Office." In *A Portrait of Marginality: The Political Behavior of the American Woman.* Ed. Marianne Githens and Jewel L. Prestage. New York: David McKay, 1977.

Lemons, J. Stanley . *The Woman Citizen: Social Feminism in the 1920s.* Urbana: University of Illinois Press, 1973.

Link, Arthur S. "What Happened to the Progressive Movement in the 1920s." *American Historical Review* 64 (1959): 833–51.

Link, Arthur S., and Richard L. McCormick. *Progressivism.* Arlington Heights, IL: Harlan Davidson, 1983.

Lippmann, Walter. "Lady Politicians: How the Old-Fashioned Illusion That Women Would Redeem Politics Has Been Destroyed." *Vanity Fair* 29 (January 1928): 43, 104.

———. *The Public Philosophy.* Boston: Little, Brown, 1955.

Logan, Edward B. "Lobbying." *Annals of the American Academy of Political Science* 144 (supplement, 1929): 32–33.

Lubbell, Samuel. *The Future of American Politics.* New York: Harper & Row, 1951.

Mansbridge, Jane. *Beyond Adversary Democracy.* New York: Basic Books, 1980.

Maisel, L. Sandy, and William G. Shade, eds. *Parties and Politics in American History.* New York: Garland Publishing, 1994.

Martin, Anne. "Feminists and Future Political Action." *Nation* 15 (18 February 1925): 185–86.

Matthews, Glenna. *The Rise of Public Woman: Woman's Power and Woman's Place in the United States, 1630–1970.* New York: Oxford University Press, 1992.

McBride, Genevieve. 1993. *On Wisconsin Women: Working for Their Rights from Settlement to Suffrage.* Madison: University of Wisconsin Press, 1993.

McCallum, Jane Y. "Activities of Women in Texas Politics." In *Texas Democracy: A Centennial History of Politics and Personalities of the Democratic Party 1836–1936.* Ed. Frank Adams. Austin: Democratic Historical Association, 1937. Reprinted in Elizabeth A. Taylor, *Citizens at Last: The Woman Suffrage Movement in Texas.* Austin: Ellen C. Temple, 1987.

McCormick, Anne O'Hare. 1928. "Enter Women, the New Boss of Politics." *New York Times Magazine,* 21 October 1928, pp. 3, 22.

McCormick, Richard L. "The Party Period and Public Policy: An Exploratory Hypothesis." *Journal of American History* 66 (September 1979): 279–98.

McGerr, Michael E. *The Decline of Popular Politics.* New York: Oxford University Press, 1986.

———. "Political Style and Women's Power, 1830–1930." *The Journal of American History* 77 (December 1990): 864–85.

McSeveney, Samuel T. "The Fourth Party System and Progressive Politics." In *Parties and Politics in American History.* Ed. L. Sandy Maisel and William G. Shade. New York: Garland Publishing, 1994.

Merriam, Charles E. *The American Party System.* New York: Macmillan, 1924.

Merriam, Charles E., and Harold F. Gosnell. *Non-Voting.* Chicago: University of Chicago Press, 1924.

Milkman, Ruth. *Gender at Work: The Dynamics of Job Segregation by Sex during World War II.* Urbana: University of Illinois Press, 1987.

Miller, Kristie. 1992. *Ruth Hanna McCormick: A Life in Politics 1880–1944.* Albuquerque: University of New Mexico Press, 1992.

Moncure, Dorothy. "Women in Political Life." *Current History* 29 (January 1929): 639–43.

Monoson, S. Sara. "The Lady and the Tiger: Women's Electoral Activism in New York City before Suffrage." *Journal of Women's History* 2 (fall 1990): 100–35.

Morrison, Glenda Eileen. "Women's Participation in the 1928 Presidential Campaign." Ph.D. thesis, University of Kansas, 1978.

Moskowitz, Belle L. "Junior Politics and Politicians." *Saturday Evening Post* 203 (6 September 1930): 6–7.

Moyer-Wing, Alice C. "The Vote: Our First Comeback." *Scribner's Magazine* 84 (September 1928): 259–64.

Muncy, Robyn. *Creating a Female Dominion in American Reform 1890–1935.* New York: Oxford University Press, 1991.

Murray, Robert. *The 103rd Ballot: Democrats and the Disaster in Madison Square Garden.* New York: Harper & Row, 1976.

National American Women's Suffrage Association. *Twenty-Five Answers to Antis.* Five-minute speeches delivered at a meeting on March 11, 1912 at the Metropolitan Temple in New York City. Later published as a booklet.

Newell, Margaretta. "Must Women Fight in Politics?" *Woman's Journal,* January 1930, pp. 10–11, 34–35.

Nichols, Carole. *Votes and More for Women: Suffrage and After in Connecticut.* Women and History 5. New York: Haworth Press, 1983.

Ogburn, William F., and Inez Goltra. "How Women Vote." *Political Science Quarterly* 34 (September 1919): 413–33.

Okin, Susan Muller. *Women in Western Political Thought.* Princeton: Princeton University Press, 1979.

————. *Justice, Gender, and the Family.* New York: Basic Books, 1991.

O'Neill, William L. *Everyone Was Brave.* Chicago: Quadrangle Books, 1969.

Parris, Judith H. *The Convention Problem.* Washington, D.C.: Brookings Institution, 1972.

Park, Maud Wood. *Front Door Lobby.* Boston: Beacon Press, 1960.

Pateman, Carole. "Women, Nature, and the Suffrage." *Ethics* 90 (July 1980): 564–75.

Peck, M.G. *Carrie Chapman Catt: A Biography.* New York: H.W. Wilson, 1944.

Perry, Elisabeth Israels. *Belle Moskowitz.* New York: Oxford University Press, 1987.

————. 1990. "The Varieties of Women's Political Influence: Voluntarism through the Women's City Club of New York, 1915–Present." Paper presented at the Conference on Women, Politics and Change, New School for Social Research, New York, NY, April 1990.

Reynolds, John F. *Testing Democracy.* Chapel Hill: University of North Carolina Press, 1988.

Rice, Stuart D., and Malcolm M. Willey. "American Women's Ineffective Use of the Vote." *Current History* 20 (1924): 641–47.

————. "A Sex Cleavage in the Presidential Election of 1920." *Journal of the American Statistical Association* 19 (1924): 519–20.

Richardson, Anna Steese. "Women at Two Conventions." *New York Times,* 7 July 1920, sec. 7, p. 2.

Rogers, Edith Nourse. "Women's New Place in Politics." *Nation's Business* 18 (August 1930): 39–41, 120, 124.

Rokkan, Stein. "The Mobilization of the Periphery: Data on Turnout, Party Membership and Candidate Recruitment in Norway." In *Citizens, Elections, Parties.* Ed. Stein Rokkan. New York: David McKay, 1970.

Roosevelt, Eleanor. "Women in Politics." *Good Housekeeping* 110 (January 1940): 18–19, 150.

———. "Women in Politics." *Good Housekeeping* 110 (March 1940): 45, 68.

———. "Women in Politics." *Good Housekeeping* 110 (April 1940): 45, 201–3.

Rosenstone, Steven J., and John Mark Hansen. *Mobilization, Participation, and Democracy in America.* New York: Macmillan, 1993.

Rusk, Jerrold G. "The Effect of The Australian Ballot Reform on Split Ticket Voting, 1876–1908." *American Political Science Review* 64 (December 1970): 1220–38.

Russell, Charles Edward. "Is Woman Suffrage a Failure?" *Century Magazine* 35 (March 1924): 724–30.

Ryan, Mary P. *Women in Public: Between Banners and Ballots, 1825–1880.* Baltimore: Johns Hopkins University Press, 1990.

Saint, Avis Marion. "Women in the Public Service: General Survey." *Public Personnel Studies* 8, no. 4 (1930): 46–54.

———. "Women in the Public Service: The City of Berkeley." *Public Personnel Studies* 8, no. 7 (1930): 104–7.

———. "Women in the Public Service: The City of Oakland." *Public Personnel Studies* 8, no. 8 (1930): 119–22.

Sapiro, Virginia. *The Political Integration of Women: Roles, Socialization, and Politics.* Urbana: University of Illinois Press, 1983.

Sarvasy, Wendy. "Beyond the Difference versus Equality Policy Debate: Postsuffrage Feminism, Citizenship, and the Quest for a Feminist Welfare State." *Signs* 17 (Winter 1992): 329–62.

Schackel, Sandra. *Social Housekeepers: Women Shaping Public Policy in New Mexico, 1920–1940.* Albuquerque: University of New Mexico Press, 1992.

Schlesinger, Arthur M., and E. M. Eriksson. "The Vanishing Voter." *New Republic* 60 (October 1924): 162–67.

Scott, Anne Firor. "After Suffrage: Southern Women in the Twenties." *Journal of Southern History* 30 (August 1964): 298–318.

———. *Natural Allies: Women's Organizations in American History.* Urbana: University of Illinois Press, 1991.

Search, Mabel. "Women's Rights in Wisconsin." *Marquette Law Review* 6 (1922): 164–69.

Sheppard, Alice. *Cartooning for Suffrage.* Albuquerque: University of New Mexico Press, 1994.

Shinn, Anne O'Hagan. 1924. "Politics Still Masculine, Convention Women Discover." *New York Times,* 29 June 1924, sec. 8, pp. 3, 11.

Silbey, Joel. "Party Organization in Nineteenth Century America." In *Parties and Politics in American History.* Ed. L. Sandy Maisel and William G. Shade. New York: Garland Publishing, 1994.

Silva, Ruth C. *Rum, Religion, and Votes: 1928 Re-Examined.* University Park: Pennsylvania State University Press, 1962.

Siltanen, Janet, and Michelle Stanworth. "The Politics of Private Woman and Public Man." In *Women and the Public Sphere*. London: Hutchinson, 1928.

Sklar, Kathryn Kish. "Historical Foundations of Women's Power in the Creation of the American Welfare State, 1830–1930." In *Mothers of a New World: Maternalist Politics and the Origins of Welfare States*. Ed. Seth Koven and Sonya Michel. New York: Routledge, 1993.

Skocpol, Theda. *Protecting Soldiers and Mothers: The Political Origins of Social Policy in the United States*. Cambridge: Harvard University Press, 1992.

Smith, Jean M. "The Voting Women of San Diego, 1920." *Journal of San Diego History* 26, no. 2 (1985): 133–54.

Stanton, Elizabeth Cady, and Susan B. Anthony. *Correspondence, Writings, Speeches*. Ed. Ellen Carol DuBois. New York: Schocken Books, 1981.

Strom, Sharon Hartman. *Beyond the Typewriter: Gender, Class, and the Origins of Modern American Office Work, 1900–1930*. Urbana: University of Illinois Press, 1992.

Sumner, Helen L. *Equal Suffrage*. New York: Harper & Brothers, 1909.

Swain, Martha H. "The Public Role of Southern Women." In *Sex, Race, and the Role of Women in the South*. Ed. Joanne V. Hawks and Sheila Skemp. Jackson: University Press of Mississippi, 1983.

Swarthout, John M. "Oregon: Political Experiment Station." In *Western Politics*. Ed. Frank H. Jonas. Salt Lake City: University of Utah Press, 1961.

Sykes, Patricia L., and Julianna S. Gonen. "The Semi-Sovereign Sex: U.S. Parties as Obstacles to the Women's Movement." Paper presented at the Annual Meeting of the Midwest Political Science Association, Chicago, IL, April 1991.

Tarbell, Ida M. "Is Woman's Suffrage a Failure?" *Good Housekeeping* 79 (October 1924): 18–19, 237–39.

Taylor, A. Elizabeth. "The Woman Suffrage Movement in North Carolina." *North Carolina Historical Review* 38 (January and April, 1961): 45–62, 173–89.

Taylor, Paul Craig. "The Entrance of Women into Party Politics: The 1920s." Ph.D. thesis, Harvard University, 1967.

Terborg-Penn, Rosalyn M. "Discontented Black Feminists: Prelude and Postscript to the Passage of the Nineteenth Amendment." In *Decades of Discontent: The Women's Movement, 1920–1940*. Ed. Lois Scharf and Joan M. Jensen. Westport, CT: Greenwood Press, 1983.

Thomas, Mary Martha. *The New Woman in Alabama: Social Reforms and Suffrage, 1890–1920*. Tuscaloosa: University of Alabama Press, 1992.

Tingsten, Herbert. *Political Behavior: Studies in Election Statistics*. London: P. S. King & Son, 1937.

Tolleson-Rinehart, Sue, and Jeanie R. Stanley. *Claytie and the Lady: Ann*

Richards, Gender, and Politics in Texas. Austin: University of Texas Press, 1994.

Toombs, E. O. "Politicians Take Notice! Columbus, Ohio Women Elected a Mayor." *Good Housekeeping* 70 (March 1929): 14–15.

Verba, Sidney, Norman H. Nie, and Jae-On Kim. *Participation and Political Equality: A Seven-Nation Study.* New York: Cambridge University Press, 1978.

Vines, Kenneth, and Henry Robert Glick. "The Impact of Universal Suffrage: A Comparison of Popular and Property Suffrage." *American Political Science Review* 61 (December 1967): 1078–87.

Wandersee, Winifred. "Frances Perkins Meets Tammany Hall: The Co-Adaptation of Machine Politics and Social Reform, 1910–1918." Paper presented at the Conference on Women, Politics and Change, New School for Social Research, April 1990.

Ware, Susan. *Beyond Suffrage: Women in the New Deal.* Cambridge: Harvard University Press, 1981.

———. *Holding Their Own: American Women in the 1930s.* Boston: Twayne Publishers, 1982.

———. *Partner and I: Molly Dewson, Feminism, and New Deal Politics.* New Haven: Yale University Press, 1987.

Weinstein, Helene E. *Lawmakers: Biographical Sketches of the Women of the New York State Legislature (1918–1988).* Albany: New York State Library, 1989.

Wells, Marguerite M. "Some Effects of Woman Suffrage." *Annals of the American Academy of Political Science* 143 (1929): 207–16.

Wheaton, Anne Williams. "The Woman Voter." *The Woman's Journal* (February 1929): 28.

Wilson, James Q. *Political Organizations.* New York: Basic Books, 1973.

Witt, Linda, Karen M. Paget, and Glenna Matthews. *Running as a Woman: Gender and Power in American Politics.* New York: Free Press, 1994.

"Woman Suffrage Declared a Failure." *Literary Digest* 81 (1924): 12–13.

Young, Louise N. "Women's Place in American Politics: the Historical Perspective." *Journal of Politics* 38 (August 1976): 295–335.

———. *In the Public Interest: The League of Women Voters, 1920–1970.* New York: Greenwood Press, 1989.

INDEX

Abbott, Grace, 136–37, 150–51, 158–59
Addams, Jane, 26, 40–41
All-female governments, 121
American Women's Suffrage Association, 77
Anderson, Mary, 37
Anthony, Susan B., 9, 77
Antiparty sentiments. *See* Party politics, critique
Anti-suffrage attitudes: political parties, 77; women's voting rates, 55–57
Anti-suffragists: voting rates, 55–56

Baker, Paula, 5, 24–25, 29–30, 33, 44, 78
Balloting. *See* Voting
Barnard, Eunice Fuller, 72
Bass, Mrs. George, 85, 93, 104
Black women: mobilization, 89; Republican clubs, 84; state legislatures, 116
Blair, Emily Newell, 38–39, 41, 46, 79, 87–88, 101, 105–9, 165
Boston: voting rates, 70; women's voting rates, 63
Breckinridge, Sophonisba, 49, 112, 115, 118–19, 125, 136–37, 146, 150–51, 154
Brown, Hallie Q., 84
Burroughs, Nannie, 84, 89
Business: gendered boundaries, 16, 19

Cable Act of 1922, 7, 27–28
Catt, Carrie Chapman: gender differences, 5, 38–39; party politics, 41, 45, 77–80, 95, 108; suffrage, 1, 3
Children's Bureau, 129, 136–37, 149–50
Citizenship: gender, 2–4, 21, 147, 169–70; gendered boundaries, 27–28, 37, 39; Progressive model, 32–33, 37. *See also* Women's citizenship
Clark, Janet, 111, 118
Clemens, Elisabeth, 4, 148–50
Contest method: men's political style, 38–39
Cott, Nancy, 2, 22, 53, 111, 147
County government: women officeholders, 119–20; women's participation, 117–18, 121

Daly, Alice Lorraine, 138
Darcy, R., 111, 118
Davis, Katherine Bement, 150–51
Democracy: cooperative nature, 36
Democratic national conventions: women as special, 98; women participants, 82–83, 87–88, 97
Democratic Party: equal representation, 84–86, 90, 93–94, 96; opposition to suffrage, 77–78; separate women's organizations, 79, 84, 87, 91, 99, 104, 109; women committee members, 85, 90; women registered voters, 65–66, 73; women voters, 65–66, 72; women's mobilization, 84–85. *See also* Party politics; Political parties; Republican Party
Democratic women: committee members, 85, 90; convention

Illinois: ethnicity, 63; women's voting
rates, 62, 65
Immigrant women: voter turnout,
72–73, 92
Indirectness. *See* Women's citizenship
Interest group politics: rise, 153;
women's organizations, 147;
women's political participation, 46

Jensen, Joan M., 66

Kelley, Florence, 137, 150
Kempfer, Mrs. Hannah, 134
Kerber, Linda, 3, 22–23
Kleppner, Paul, 10, 74–75
Knapp, Mrs. Florence, 127
Kraditor, Aileen, 22
Ku Klux Klan, 65

LaFollette, Fola, 112
Lathrop, Julia, 129, 137, 150–51
League of Women Voters, 38; 1924
convention, 41–42; candidate forums, 12, 27, 105, 145; Catt's
speech, 95; citizenship, 37; first national meeting, 39; lobbying, 8;
nonpartisanship, 44–45; political
education, 35–36, 69, 135–36; radio broadcasts, 71
Lebsock, Suzanne, 9
Legislative accomplishments: women,
8–9, 154–55
Lemons, J. Stanley, 7, 28, 155–56, 158,
166
Lilly, Mrs. May, 96–97
Lippman, Walter, 31, 161
Lobbying: impact on politics, 161;
women's organizations, 8, 148–49,
158–59
Local government: all-female, 121;
women appointees, 146; women officeholders, 119; women's participation, 117–18
Lufkin, Winifred, 124

Male party leaders: resistance to
women, 92–94, 104–5
Martin, Anne, 77, 108
Matthews, Glenna, 5

McCormick, Ruth Hanna: candidacy,
124, 136; in Congress, 113; party
politics, 41–42, 81; personal ambition, 139, 165; political education,
164; political women's network,
151–52; political education, 102;
political resources, 96; women's citizenship, 35
Men's citizenship: public perception,
22, 24, 27
Men's domain, 13; public sphere, 12
Men's political participation: contest
method, 38–39; motivation, 36–37
Men's politics: entry of women, 5; public sphere, 3; women's participation, 13
Merriam, Charles E., 31, 53, 55,
58–59, 75
Minority parties: women candidates,
114, 124, 126; women delegates, 79
Monoson, S. Sara, 2n.1, 26
Moral authority: women, 3, 5, 13, 25,
27, 33, 36–37
Moral house-cleaning: women in local
government, 133–34; women officeholders, 135
Moskowitz, Belle, 37, 88–89, 100,
128–29, 162
Mother's Club of Cambridge, 26
Muncy, Robyn, 8, 136, 155, 159, 168
Municipal housekeeping: political
women, 128; politics, 164; women
candidates, 138; women in local
government, 133–34; women's organizations, 4; women's policy
agenda, 104; women's public activities, 13, 26

National American Woman Suffrage
Association, 39
National Association of Colored
Women, 84
National League of Republican Col-
ored Women, 84, 89
National Women's Suffrage Associa-
tion, 77
New Mexico: women reformers, 152–
54; women's voting rates, 66, 90,
96